READING AND WRITING
Across Content Areas

Roberta Sejnost & Sharon Thiese

PEARSON
SkyLight
Glenview, Illinois

Reading and Writing Across Content Areas

Published by Pearson Professional Development
1900 E. Lake Ave., Glenview, IL 60025
800-348-4474 or 847-657-7450
Fax 847-486-3183
info@skylightedu.com
http://www.skylightedu.com

LCCN 00-109602
ISBN 1-57517-362-X

2794-V

ZYXWVUTSRQPONMLKJIHGFE
08 07 06 05 04 03   15 14 13 12 11 10 9 8 7 6 5

READING AND WRITING
Across Content Areas

Dedication

We dedicate this book to Drew, Emma, Jonathon, and Claire (and any other grandchildren who may come along), for they are the future learners of our world; may this book provide their teachers with strategies to make them and others like them lifelong learners.

—Roberta Sejnost and Sharon Thiese

Contents

Acknowledgments

There are several people who deserve a great big thanks for supporting and believing in me; they are the ones who gave me the courage and perseverance to complete this book. My deepest thanks go to my mother, Edna, who taught me the love of reading and the appreciation for learning; my dad, Joe, God rest his soul, who taught me that perfection is everything; my husband, Art, who always lets me "do it my way" and continues to love me no matter what; my daughters, Sheryl and Melissa, who believe I can do anything and spur me on when I think I can't; my co-author, Sharon, who stuck by my side, offered her wisdom and clear thinking, and exhibited infinite patience; and Sue Schumer, our editor, whose kind words and gentle nature guided us as we wrote.

—Roberta Sejnost

I want to thank Robin Fogarty for encouraging me to write this book and our editor, Sue Schumer, for her guidance and patience throughout the whole process. I am indebted to Roberta for her willingness to work with me and for sharing her expertise as a teacher; to my mom who taught me to value education; to my colleague, Vicky Landberg; to my sister, Johneen, for listening to me and giving me feedback; and to my husband, Jim, for his support.

—Sharon Thiese

Introduction

Reading and writing are tools that enable students to acquire knowledge in their content area classes. Yet, teachers are often frustrated when they try to meet their students' needs only to find their instructional plans impeded by their students' failure to comprehend their textbooks efficiently or to express their ideas in writing effectively. Thus, a prime concern of educators today is how to help students become competent learners by using reading and writing to acquire knowledge in the various content areas. Furthermore, current research on the learning process and the prevalence of technology in our society emphasize the need for teachers to instruct students in ways that will ensure that learning occurs for all.

This book presents research-based best practices related to reading and writing and offers content area strategies that integrate reading and writing and utilize technology. These strategies are based on the theory of multiple intelligences and brain-based research, which can be applied in every classroom, no matter what the subject or grade level. Examples and blackline masters of the strategies are included in this book, as well as suggestions for assessment tools and technology-related activities that assure immediate transfer to all content area classrooms.

Chapter 1 (Creating the Framework for Reading) explains the importance of matching readers with the text and describes methods to help students interpret a text as well as identify key patterns of text structure for reading. In addition, it offers ideas for students to become proficient in graphic literacy.

Chapter 2 (Setting the Framework for Writing) reviews all phases of the writing process and defines terms important to understanding the elements of writing such as *audience* and *lead*.

Chapter 3 (Keying into Vocabulary) discusses the principles of effective vocabulary instruction, giving specific examples of teacher-centered and student-centered strategies.

Chapter 4 (Strategies for Comprehension) identifies the characteristics of a strategic reader, explains the reading process, and illustrates specific examples of prereading, during reading, and after reading strategies.

Chapter 5 (Research Writing) reviews basic research skills and describes nontraditional and traditional forms of research.

Chapter 6 (Integrating Reading and Writing in the Classroom) presents effective strategies and examples to foster prior knowledge and critical understanding, to engage readers and writers in the process of revision, and to encourage all students to become personally involved in their learning.

Chapter 7 (Assessing Reading and Writing) describes formal assessments in reading and writing and provides suggestions for alternative assessments as well as test taking strategies and study strategies for good test performance.

Overall, *Reading and Writing Across Content Areas* is designed to be teacher-friendly, so that literacy is achieved in every classroom and students can, indeed, become lifelong learners.

CHAPTER 1

Creating the Framework for Reading

Never let the future disturb you. You will meet it, if you have to, with the same weapons of reason which today arm you against the present. . . .

Marcus Aurelius

CONTENT AREA LITERACY

MATCHING THE READER AND THE TEXT
- The Raygor Readability Formula*
- The Cloze Procedure
- Readability Checklist*

INTERPRETING THE TEXT
- Question-Answer Relationship Strategy (QARS)
- Content Area Reading Inventory (CARI)

PATTERNS OF TEXT STRUCTURE FOR READING
- Definition/Example Text Structure
- Proposition/Support Text Structure
- Comparison/Contrast Text Structure
- Cause/Effect Text Structure
- Problem/Solution Text Structure

GRAPHIC LITERACY
- Graphs
- Tables
- Maps
- Graphic Information Lesson

CHAPTER SUMMARY

*Indicates that a Blackline Master is included in Teacher Tips at the end of the chapter.

Creating the
Framework
for Reading

Setting the
Framework
for Writing

Keying into
Vocabulary

Strategies for
Comprehension

Research
Writing

Integrating
Reading and
Writing in
the Classroom

Assessing
Reading
and Writing

CONTENT AREA LITERACY

Content area literacy, according to McKenna and Robinson (1990), is the ability to use reading and writing in order to learn new content material in a given subject area—a complicated process indeed. They note that content literacy is not the same as content knowledge because content literacy requires students to possess (a) general literacy skills, (b) content-specific literacy skills—the ability to read maps, charts, and graphs, and (c) prior knowledge of the content being studied. However, they do stress that content knowledge is a prerequisite of content literacy. Obviously, the more a person knows about a content, the more that knowledge will aid in the reading and writing of that content. McKenna and Robinson are quick to point out that content area teachers do not need to actually teach reading and writing. Rather, as students acquire content literacy skills, they read and write to learn rather than learn to read and write.

Another notion McKenna and Robinson present is that content literacy is content specific. In other words, students may be literate in one content but not so literate in another. Those who have difficulty programming their VCRs will certainly attest to this truth since they are probably not "technologically literate." Finally, McKenna and Robinson stress that the concept of content literacy presents some serious implications for classroom use because, in the mission to help students achieve content literacy, teachers must realize that reading and writing are complementary tasks. As a result, teachers must set expectations for content literacy high enough to challenge students.

Almost every day we open a newspaper or hear a news broadcast that decries the current standards of literacy in the United States. In 1998 the US Department of Education's Office of Educational Research and Improvement provided some dismal news about literacy in its 1998 National Assessment of Educational Progress (NAEP) Reading Report Card. This report is issued every four years and portrays nationwide student achievement in reading at grades four, eight, and twelve.

NAEP, a congressionally mandated project of the US Department of Education's National Center for Education Statistics, has assessed the academic performance of students at grades four, eight, and twelve in a variety of subjects including reading, writing, and mathematics since 1969. This report provides descriptions of students' strengths and weaknesses in basic and higher-order skills as well as comparisons of achievement by race/ethnicity, gender, community, regions, and trends across the years.

The NAEP reading assessment measures the reading comprehension of students. In addition to assessing their ability to understand the three purposes of reading (for literary experience, to gain information, and to perform a task), it also assesses the four different approaches readers take in trying to comprehend what is read. These responses include: forming an initial understanding of the text, developing an interpretation of the text, personally responding to the text, and taking a critical stance.

Although the 1998 average reading score was higher than the 1992 score at the eighth grade level, there was no net gain seen over the 1992 average scores for students in fourth and twelfth grades. While these scores are alarming, there is even more cause for concern when we look at these data in relation to their impact on academic performance in school. The NAEP performance achievement levels are reported in three categories: Basic, Proficient, and Advanced. The Proficient Level represents an ability to show solid academic performance and is the level of achievement identified as a standard that all students should reach. Students who achieve this level are considered competent enough to read challenging subject matter, apply the knowledge gained to real-world situations, and use analytical skills appropriate to the subject matter (Office of Educational Research and

I can't wait until this comes out in a book.

Improvement, US Department of Education 1998). Unfortunately, the 1998 NAEP report reveals that this level was achieved by only 31 percent of fourth grade students; 33 percent of eighth grade students; and 40 percent of twelfth grade students!

Given this information, many observers cannot help but wonder if we are headed for an Age of Illiteracy. Since the NAEP report describes changes in student achievement as measured through the long-term assessment in reading, we have reason for concern. The 1998 report findings indicate that almost 70 percent of fourth and eighth grade students and 60 percent of twelfth grade students will not effectively function in college or in the work setting in the future. They may not be able to read and understand test directions, instructions for operating machinery, office memos, tax forms, and so on. In addition, because of their inability to read, they may not know how to gain access to that information. As a result, many fear that the unemployment rate might rise, forcing young people into low-paying jobs and necessitating remedial programs.

As we reflect on this notion, we also become aware that the concept of literacy itself seems to have an ambiguous shape. What does it mean to be literate today? Does it mean the same thing that it did a century ago? Roberta Sejnost's grandmother sometimes reminisces about her immigration from Czechoslovakia. She tells a wonderful story about how she and her husband were channeled into the "literate line" when they landed at Ellis Island. Since they could each identify their names and were able to sign their names on a baggage receipt, they were considered literate! Perhaps in the late 1800s that was all that was needed to be literate, but that definition surely would not stand today!

Today literacy seems to be a complex, multifaceted creature. On a regular basis, we hear terms such as *computer literacy,* the ability to use a computer and software to accomplish simple tasks; *cultural literacy,* the ability to read about another population and understand their customs and beliefs; *media literacy,* the ability to understand communication in various mass media; *visual literacy,* the ability to understand graphic material such as charts and maps; and *academic literacy,* the ability to read and understand the academic texbooks used in classrooms. In addition, McKenna and Robinson (1990) speak of *content literacy,* the kind of literacy that we feel most affects our students in their daily learning activities and nationwide assessments such as the NAEP.

MATCHING THE READER AND THE TEXT

As we work to make our students literate, we utilize many tools, the major one being a textbook. In fact, Zahorik (1991) estimates that during the school years, students utilize texts in some fashion from 55 to 91 percent of the time. Yet, we as teachers know that the reading of texts often presents problems for our students. We hear them complain that the books are too difficult as well as boring and dry. Even worse, many profess that they simply do not understand what they have read. And, when this is the case, students become frustrated and simply give up, not bothering to read their texts at all.

To understand how your students feel, read the following paragraph:

> When the computer functions are suspended, a fatal error is caused. In order to repair the problem you may be required to halt the process. Holding down the control, alt, and delete keys simultaneously will end the task. It might also prove useful to defrag the system afterward.

Was this snippet of text easy to understand? Would you have understood it better had you a command of the content-specific vocabulary used? Do you fare better with the next example?

> I spent forty-five minutes in eyeball hang time, and I only made one hit!

Both of these samples make perfect sense to someone who is computer literate but may well stymie those who are not. Thus, we must admit that these text samples are not very meaningful or user-friendly to readers who are unacquainted with computer terminology.

When we look at texts, then, we need to consider the subject of readability. Harris and Hodges (1995) note that readability is really a measure of how easily a text can be read based on the style of writing used. These researchers point out that variables in the text (such as format, typography, content, literary form and style, vocabulary difficulty, sentence complexity, concept load, and cohesiveness) contribute to whether or not the text can be easily understood. When variables within the student (such as motivation, reading ability, background knowledge, and interests) come into play, the issue of readability becomes even more complex. Richardson and Morgan (1997) warn us that readability is not just a formula but, instead, a combination of the characteristics within the reader and those within the text. Furthermore, they suggest that it is only by considering the notion of readability that teachers will be able to prepare their students to read and learn.

This leads to the question of what we can do to determine whether or not our students are well matched to the texts they use. How can we determine if the text is written at the appropriate reading level? Research dating from the 1920s until now reports that, on the whole, textbooks are written at levels that well exceed students' reading abilities (Chall and Squire 1991). Secondly, how do we determine whether our students have enough prior knowledge to understand the text? Chall (1947) tested sixth and eighth grade students and discovered that the students' prior knowledge about a topic was positively correlated to their comprehension of a passage on that topic. Students who had the highest knowledge scores also succeeded in achieving the highest comprehension scores. Finally, since we know that students are better able to comprehend a text that is well written and filled with frequent examples and graphic aids (Readence, Bean, and Baldwin 1998), is there an overall analysis teachers can use to determine whether the text they choose is user-friendly? In the following sections, we provide an explanation of three methods: the readability formula, the cloze procedure, and the textbook analysis. These methods help teachers determine how well their students' ability levels correlate with the texts they must read.

The Raygor Readability Formula

There are probably more than 100 readability formulas currently in use today. They are widely used by teachers and administrators as a way of predicting if a text is written at a level appropriate for the students who will use it. While we can say with relative ease that readability formulas are fairly reliable, we need to be cautious in using them. As Richardson and Morgan (1997) point out, readability formulas are useful when textbook selection committees need to make a decision but have no students available to try out the materials on, or when teachers want to assess materials that students may be asked to read independently. Basically, a readability formula is a quick and easy way to determine the grade level of written material. However, we must remember that it is only one measure, and the grade level obtained is only a predictor and, thus, may not be exact (Richardson and Morgan 1997). Harris and Hodges (1995) provide the following suggestions to predict readability accurately:

1. Consider the purpose of getting a readability score. Texts used to cultivate readers should be more challenging than those used to merely inform or entertain them.

2. Choose the formula carefully and consider the formula's screening devices and all scores' probability statements.

3. Choose a formula that yields two index variables—semantic and syntactic.

4. Take a large random sample of the text in order to increase the accuracy of the analysis, to ascertain the reliability of the average score, and to get an indication of variability.

5. Be aware that different readability formulas often give different grade level scores.

6. Remember that readability formulas are derived from counts of style variables. They can be poor predictors in upper grade level texts where content weighs heavily.

7. Do not rely on readability formulas alone. Take into account students' abilities, motivation levels, and prior knowledge. Also, seek the opinion of experts, or seek the consensus opinions of colleagues.

As noted earlier, the numbers of readability formulas available are impressive. One that is both simple and reliable, since it eliminates the step of counting syllables and replaces it with counting words of six or more letters, is the Raygor Readability Estimate (Raygor 1977). Anyone who has ever battled with the task of counting syllables (a common step in most gauges of readability such as the Fry, SMOG, and FOG formulas) is cognizant of how easily a counting error can be made. Of course, if an error occurs, the reliability of the formula is compromised. The Raygor Readability Estimate eliminates this margin of error by counting words of six letters or more rather than by counting syllables. Furthermore, Baldwin and Kaufman (1979) point out that while both the Raygor and the Fry yield similar readability estimates, the Raygor is much easier and faster to use, elements every busy classroom teacher will appreciate (see Figure 1.1). See Teacher Tips at the end of this chapter for a Blackline Master of the Raygor Readability Graph (Figure 1.7).

Sample Raygor Readability Graph

Directions: Choose three 100-word passages, one at the beginning, one in the middle, and one at the end of the textbook. In the count, include proper nouns, but do not include numbers. Then follow these steps:

   a. Count the number of sentences in each passage, estimating to the nearest tenth.
   b. Count the words that have six or more letters.
   c. Average the sentence length and the word length over three samples. Then plot the average on the graph.

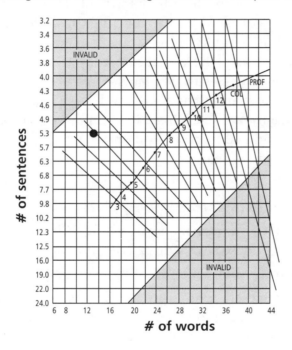

Example:

	Sentences	Number of Words (with Six or More Letters)
Sample A	5	10
Sample B	5.6	15
Sample C	5.2	12
TOTAL	15.8	37
AVERAGE	5.3	12.3

According to the figures calculated, the text is written at the fifth grade level.

Figure 1.1

The Cloze Procedure

Although a readability formula is certainly useful in estimating the difficulty of a textbook and indicating the reading level students must possess to comprehend the material, it focuses on variables in the text such as sentence length, word length, or number of syllables used. The formula fails, however, to take into consideration reader variables such as student experience, interest, motivation, prior knowledge, or knowledge of content vocabulary. The Cloze Procedure (Taylor 1953) is a method that measures how well students can comprehend a selection based on how they interact with the reading material. "Closure" takes place when the reader is able to supply enough of the deleted words to understand the passage.

In effect, as students move through a "cloze" passage—reading actively, thinking, and filling in blanks appropriately—they must make use of their prior knowledge and manipulate their knowledge of content-based vocabulary as well as the author's style of writing. Richardson and Morgan (1977) suggest steps for constructing the cloze for all grade levels as well as a method of interpreting scores (see Figure 1.2). If students score at 60 percent or above on the measure, they are considered capable of reading the text independently. Students who score between 40 percent and 60 percent are at an instructional level and will be able to read the text with assistance from the teacher. Finally, those who score below 40 percent are at a frustrational level and will find the material simply too difficult to comprehend or learn.

 Steps in Constructing a Cloze

1. Select a passage of approximately 125 words for students in grades 1–3. Choose a passage of 250–300 words for students in grades 4–12.

2. Copy the first sentence of the passage in its entirety.

3. Delete every tenth word, until a total of ten words are deleted for students in grades 1–3 and every fifth word until a total of fifty words are deleted for students in grades 4–12.

4. Copy the last sentence in its entirety. (You may, for continuity, copy the remainder of the paragraph.)

5. For students in grades 1–3, create a word bank containing the exact words that have been deleted. (However, **do not** list the words in the order they appear in the text.)

6. For students in grades 4–12, instruct students to read the passage, filling in each blank with the exact word they believe was deleted. (Note: Research indicates that the most valid score is reached when the exact word is used.)

7. To score, calculate the number of correct responses and multiply by 10 for students in grades 1–3 and by 2 for students in grades 4–12 to determine percentage.

Figure 1.2 will help you determine the instructional match between the text and your students and provide some insight into how successfully your students will comprehend the text.

Levels of Comprehension as Assessed by the Cloze Procedure		
Independent Level	**Instructional Level**	**Frustrational Level**
Score 60% or Above	**Score Between 40% and 60%**	**Score Below 40%**
Text is easy for the student; it can be read independently without instructional aid from a teacher.	Text is suitable for the student; it can be comprehended easily with instructional aid from a teacher.	Text is too difficult for the student; the text may require modification. An alternative text may need to be assigned or a great deal of instructional guidance may need to be provided by a teacher.

Figure 1.2

Following is an example of the Cloze Procedure you could use in your science classroom.

EXAMPLE OF THE CLOZE PROCEDURE FOR SCIENCE

Passage

The body contains several systems that keep it functioning well. While all of these 1.___ are crucial to the 2.___ survival, we will discuss 3.___ of them: the digestive 4.___, the circulatory system, and 5.___ respiratory system.

There are 6.___ organs in the digestive 7.___: the stomach, the small 8.___, and the liver. Their 9.___ purpose is to process 10.___ we all eat. However, 11.___ bodies can only use 12.___ we eat after the 13.___ system does its work 14.___ allowing enzymes and digestive 15.___ to change the food 16.___ chemical forms that are 17.___ by the body. Then, 18.___ food undergoes this chemical 19.___, it then moves to 20.___ bloodstream, and at this 21.___ the circulatory system begins 22.___ important job.

In the 23.___ system, the heart is the 24.___ worker. It works hard 25.___ pump the blood through 26.___ body's veins, arteries, and 27.___. During this very complex 28.___, the blood works to 29.___ the food to the 30.___ cells. At the same time, 31.___ also removes the wastes. 32.___ function of the blood 33.___ to produce antibodies which 34.___ the special agents that 35.___ the body's cells against 36.___.

The respiratory system is 37.___ unique system that keeps 38.___ breathing. Air, which contains 39.___, moves in and out 40.___ our bodies regularly. It 41.___ enters through our nasal 42.___ or mouths. Next, the 43.___ passes into our throats 44.___ down our windpipes where 45.___ eventually enters our lungs. 46.___ in the lungs, the 47.___ proceeds to absorb the 48.___ and then gives off 49.___ dioxide as a by-product 50.___ the process.

This, then, is a thumbnail sketch of three of the several systems that our body has. Each and every one of them is truly a miracle in operation!

Answers:

1. systems	11. our	21. point	31. it	41. usually
2. body's	12. food	22. its	32. Another	42. passages
3. three	13. digestive	23. circulatory	33. is	43. air
4. system	14. by	24. major	34. are	44. and
5. the	15. juices	25. to	35. guard	45. it
6. three	16. into	26. the	36. disease	46. Once
7. system	17. utilized	27. capillaries	37. the	47. blood
8. intestine	18. the	28. process	38. us	48. oxygen
9. basic	19. change	29. deliver	39. oxygen	49. carbon
10. foods	20. the	30. body's	40. of	50. of

The Readability Checklist

Although readability formulas and cloze procedures provide some excellent and valuable information about how well our students can understand their textbooks, there is another procedure to help us determine the text's usability, the Readability Checklist. Basically, we know a textbook that is efficiently and effectively written will be easier for students to understand. Common sense tells us that students will better comprehend a text they can understand and use easily. In other words, when considering textbooks, we must consider such questions as: Is the text well organized? Does it have a table of contents? An index? Does each chapter begin with an introduction and end with a summary? Do the chapter titles and subheadings provide a clear outline of the material to be read? Are the ideas and concepts presented logically? Are main ideas stated clearly and with adequate, but not superfluous, supporting details? Do the visual aids adequately reflect the content they represent? Is important vocabulary highlighted and supported with effective context clues or a glossary? These are just a few of the questions we need to consider when we choose a text for our students.

There are numerous readability checklists available for use to help teachers evaluate texts. However, one we find most utilitarian is the Readability Checklist developed by Irwin and Davis (1980). See Teacher Tips at the end of this chapter for a Blackline Master of the Readability Checklist (Figure 1.6).

INTERPRETING THE TEXT

Once we are confident that students are able to read the words in their textbooks with comfort, we also must be sure that they are equipped with the processes to maneuver through the text with ease and to answer the text-based questions we ask them. Too often we hear our students complain that they have been given questions for which they cannot locate the answers. Unfortunately, much of the time they are correct. Yet this is not the fault of the teachers who pose the questions; the fault is really a two-fold problem.

First, most of our students recognize only one type of question—the textually explicit question that is found easily in one place in the text. Often, obvious markers such as boldface type lead the reader to a definition that is readily located. However, as teachers, we also expect our students to ascend in the hierarchy of thought and answer questions that are textually implicit. To answer these questions, they must think about and peruse several sections of the text. In addition, they must process, apply, and transfer their thoughts about these difficult questions to real-life experiences.

The second part of the problem lies in the fact that many of our students do not familiarize themselves with their texts, and too often teachers do not do an effective job of introducing these texts. We would never buy a house without walking through it first, or a car without going for a test drive. Yet we expect students to open their books and jump right into the text without ever bothering to introduce them to the format.

Question-Answer Relationship Strategy (QARS)

These two problems can be alleviated, however, by using the Question-Answer Relationship Strategy and Content Area Reading Inventories. Teaching students to identify various kinds of questions as explicit or implicit in the text can help them to both locate and synthesize information. Raphael (1984, 1986) illustrated four types of questions in her Question-Answer Relationship Strategy (QARS) shown in Figure 1.3.

The Question-Answer Relationship Strategy (QARS)		
Kind of Question	**Textually Explicit or Implicit**	**Characteristics**
Right There	Explicit	Answer stated directly in the text.
Think and Search	Implicit	Answer requires students to put together several sections of the text.
Author and You	Implicit and Explicit	Answer requires that students mesh their thoughts about a topic with information the author presents.
On Your Own	Implicit	Answer comes from application of the information from the text.

Figure 1.3

 Steps for the QARS Strategy

1. Introduce the concept of QARS by explaining each type, providing a clear example, and discussing the difference in each.
2. Assign students a short piece of text to read.

3. Upon completion of the reading, lead the students through the process of answering each type of question, making sure they go back into the text to verify their answers. Ascertain that they clearly understand the differences among each type.

4. Continue this practice, increasing the number of questions for each type until students are clearly able to understand the differences among the types and can identify them with ease.

5. Finally, ask students to read a longer passage and develop a set of QARS for their classmates to identify and answer.

Once students have become accustomed to the QARS format, apply the strategy to content area assignments and discussion sessions. In classrooms in which students have learned to use QARS, teachers can often be heard telling a student who is having difficulty locating an answer to a question: "It is a Think and Search Question," or "It is an On Your Own Question." That is usually all it takes to get a response of "Ohhh! Now I get it!" See the following examples of this useful strategy.

EXAMPLE OF QARS FOR SOCIAL STUDIES

Children and Immigration

Right There Questions

1. How long were immigrant children required to go to school?
2. In what year did the first school for immigrant children open?

Think and Search Questions

1. What kinds of jobs were available for immigrant boys?
2. How did the teachers treat the immigrant children?

Author and You Questions

1. Identify some ways that the immigrants' new and old countries were similar.
2. How did the immigrant experience make most children feel?

On Your Own Questions

1. If you were an immigrant child, what would have been most difficult about coming to America?
2. What could have been done to make the immigrant children's lives more comfortable?

EXAMPLE OF QARS FOR SCIENCE

Planet Uranus

Right There Questions

1. How long is a year on Uranus?
2. Name the five moons of Uranus.

Think and Search Questions

1. How is Uranus different from Earth?
2. What caused the surface features of Uranus' moons?

Author and You Questions

1. How were scientists able to learn new information about Uranus?
2. Why do you think that Uranus is called a dark planet?

On Your Own Questions

1. Do you think there is life on Uranus? Explain your answer.
2. Describe what you think life on Uranus would be like.

Content Area Reading Inventory (CARI)

A Content Area Reading Inventory (CARI) is an excellent and easy way to judge how successfully students can learn from their content area texts. This inventory is an informal, silent measure that can be easily administered to the entire class within a single class period. Furthermore, since it is a teacher-made measure constructed using the students' actual content area textbook, the diagnostic information garnered is both informative and relevant. Teachers can easily assess which areas of the text or which skills and strategies may provide potential problems for students. Finally, the fact that the measure is teacher-made offers students the opportunity of becoming familiar with the style of writing the teacher uses to compose questions.

Readance, Bean, and Baldwin (1998) suggest that an effective CARI consists of three major sections. The first section assesses students' knowledge of and ability to utilize the various textual and reading aids such as the table of contents, glossary, index, pictures, charts, maps, and graphs. Ability to use these aids is tantamount to successfully learning the content of the textbook. The next two sections require students to read portions of the text and then respond. In section two, students respond to questions that assess their knowledge and use of the technical or specialized vocabulary pertinent to the content. In section three, students respond to explicit and implicit comprehension questions as well as questions that reflect their ability to manipulate text structure. Vacca and Vacca (1996) suggest that a fourth section, rate of reading, be added.

 ### Steps for Content Area Reading Inventory

1. Select a short passage (2–6 pages) from the class text for students to read.

2. Construct approximately 20–25 questions based on the text material read using the following format.

   a. Construct 8–10 questions about using the study and reading aids found in the text, such as the table of contents, index, glossary, chapter introductions, and summaries, and visual aids, such as charts, maps, graphs, and pictures. Include questions about reference texts like encyclopedias, the *Readers' Guide to Periodical Literature*, and common library technological search tools.

   b. Construct 4–6 questions on content specific vocabulary.

   c. Construct 7–9 questions testing both explicit and implicit textual information that indicate students' abilities to make sense of the book's structure.

   d. In order to inventory reading rate, have students record how long it took them to read the selection and then ask them to divide the number of words read by the number of minutes it took them to read. This will result in a words-per-minute score.

   e. Score the test according to your criteria. Readance, Bean, and Baldwin (1998) suggest the following:

Percent Correct	Range of Text Difficulty
86–100%	Text is too easy; student can work at Independent Level.
64–85%	Text is adequate for instruction; student can work at Instructional Level.
63% and below	Text is too difficult; student is working at Frustrational Level.

   f. In discussing the CARI results with students, be sure to help them see the relationship between their reading rate and their vocabulary and comprehension scores.

   g. Finally, use the results of the CARI to determine areas students have mastered and those in which they will need further instruction.

See the following for an example of a Content Area Reading Inventory.

EXAMPLE OF CONTENT AREA READING INVENTORY FOR SCIENCE

Section I : Study and Reading Aids

1. On what page would you find a map of the solar system?
   (Tests ability to find a map or table in a science textbook.)

2. On what page does chapter 7 begin? What is the title of the unit that contains this chapter?
   (Tests ability to use table of contents.)

3. How can the introduction on page 18 and the summary on page 49 help you to study the chapter?
   (Tests understanding of unit introduction and chapter summary.)

4. Why are the chapter questions and vocabulary exercises on pages 50–53 valuable?
   (Tests understanding of specific study aids.)

5. What library aid tells you the call number of a book on plant mutation?
   (Tests knowledge of library information resources.)

6. Name a library guide that will help you find information about a famous scientist.
   (Tests knowledge of reference materials.)

7. Name a library guide that will help you find current information about cloning.
   (Tests knowledge of reference materials.)

8. Look at the chart on page 32. From the information given, tell what the jobs of the specific cell parts are.
   (Tests ability to understand charts.)

9. Look at the map on page 69. From the information given, tell which of the following are found near the picture of the city: a river, a school, hills, train tracks, major roadway, dirt road.
   (Tests ability to understand maps.)

Section II: Vocabulary

10. Define *nucleus*.

11. Read the third paragraph on page 31. From the information given in that paragraph, what do you think a nuclear membrane is?

12. What is a vacuole?

13. Give an example of diffusion.

Section III: Text Explicit and Text Implicit Information

14. What six elements make up most of the living matter of our earth? (Text explicit)

15. What do chloroplasts contain? (Text explicit)

16. Why are mitochondria often called the powerhouses of the cells? (Text implicit)

17. How do mitochondria and chloroplasts differ? (Text implicit)

18. What is found between the cell membrane and the nucleus? (Text explicit)

19. Read the section entitled "Cells and Their Jobs." Create a mind map or an outline that clearly illustrates the cells and the specific jobs they do. (Text implicit)

PATTERNS OF TEXT STRUCTURE FOR READING

As readers and writers ourselves, we are aware that information in textbooks is organized according to a hierarchy, where ideas are layered according to importance: first, ideas that represent major concepts; second, ideas that are subordinate to these major concepts; and finally, ideas that relate to the subordinating ideas. This hierarchy is often referred to as the text structure or text organizational pattern. Textbook authors use many different basic patterns of organization in their writing, but, in our experience, we have found that five patterns are used consistently: (1) definition/example; (2) proposition/support; (3) comparison/contrast; (4) cause/effect; (5) problem/solution. Research

The teacher is right! It IS easier to understand a book if you create a movie in your mind about the content.

shows that students who are able to recognize and use an author's text structure/organization are able to comprehend their content area textbooks much more effectively than students who cannot (Armbruster, Anderson, and Ostertag 1989; Taylor and Samuels 1983). Thus, it seems only wise to make all students aware of the text structure and organizational patterns authors use so they can utilize this knowledge to better comprehend their content area textbooks.

The challenge we face as teachers, then, is to effectively teach these patterns to students. Armbruster and Anderson (1985) use the phrase *text frames* to refer to those key questions and categories of information that align themselves with the specific text patterns authors use to present their information. Buehl (1995) developed a series of questions to help students of all grade levels identify each of these paragraph patterns more efficiently.

Definition/Example Text Structure

Consider the following questions as you read.

What is the concept?

To what category does it belong?

What are its critical characteristics or attributes?

How does it work?

What does it do?

What are its functions?

What are examples of it?

What are some examples of things that share some but not all of its characteristics?

Definition/Example Text Structure Questions from *Classroom Strategies for Interactive Learning* by Doug Buehl (1995), Wisconsin State Reading Association. Reprinted with permission of the Wisconsin State Reading Association.

The following shows how the definition/example text strategy is used.

EXAMPLE OF DEFINITION/EXAMPLE TEXT STRUCTURE

Learning Doesn't End at Three O'Clock

A comprehensive high school is a place where adolescents can receive a well-rounded education in academics and life. To develop academically, students have the opportunity to enroll in a variety of classes. They can study subjects that provide a basic, educational foundation like language arts, mathematics, and science as well as subjects that will prepare them for future vocations such as auto mechanics, word processing, and fashion merchandising. In addition, they also have a choice of subjects that will enhance their cultural side, such as foreign languages, art, music, and even cinema! But their education does not stop there. A comprehensive high school also offers students an opportunity to develop life skills. Diverse extracurricular activities like Math Club, Photography Club, Outdoor Adventure Club, and Latin Dance Club give students an opportunity to practice their social skills while honing their specific interests. Organized athletic programs allow them to practice their competitive skills and achieve their personal best. Truly, a comprehensive high school can offer many things to students eager to take advantage of the array of activities offered!

Proposition/Support Text Structure

Consider the following questions as you read.

What is the general topic area or issue?

What proposition (viewpoint, theory, hypothesis, thesis) is being presented?

How is the proposition being supported?

Are examples provided? Do the examples support the proposition?

Are data provided? Do the data support the proposition?

Is expert verification provided? Does it support the proposition?

Is a logical argument provided? Does it support the proposition?

Is a sufficient case presented to warrant acceptance of the proposition?

Proposition/Support Text Structure Questions from *Classroom Strategies for Interactive Learning* by Doug Buehl (1995), Wisconsin State Reading Association. Reprinted by permission of the Wisconsin State Reading Association.

See the following for a useful example of proposition/support text structure.

EXAMPLE OF PROPOSITION/SUPPORT TEXT STRUCTURE

Four Years of Fun

There are many reasons why high school can be an enjoyable experience for adolescents. First, even though teens must attend classes, passing in the halls between those classes can provide opportunities for seeing friends and sharing a few minutes of gossip, jokes, or just plain old moral support. Next, lunch provides a much needed break in a busy day. During a lunch break of close to an hour, friends can eat, talk, relax, laugh, and even help each other with a little bit of last-minute homework. It is also a perfect time to find out what algebra homework was assigned or, even more importantly, how hard the chemistry test was! And, best of all, the cafeteria is the place where all the candy and pop machines are; junk food can make any experience loads of fun. Last, but not least, are the after-school activities. When the long academic day ends, some students eagerly look forward to athletic practices, club meetings, and play or band practice. Many students fill their weekends with athletic competitions and concerts and dances. There is no doubt in my mind: high school is fun and getting better every day!

Comparison/Contrast Text Structure

Consider the following questions as you read.

What is being compared/contrasted?

What categories of characteristics or attributes are used to compare/contrast these things?

How are things alike or similar?

How are the things not alike or different?

What are the most important qualities or attributes that make them similar?

What are the most important qualities or attributes that make them different?

In terms of the qualities that are most important, are these things more alike or more different?

What can we conclude about these things or items?

Comparison/Contrast Text Structure Questions from *Classroom Strategies for Interactive Learning* by Doug Buehl (1995), Wisconsin State Reading Association. Reprinted with permission of the Wisconsin State Reading Association.

See the following for a useful example of contrast text structure.

EXAMPLE OF CONTRAST TEXT STRUCTURE

A World Apart

There are many differences between middle school and high school. The biggest difference is in the number of people who attend each. Most middle schools have a hundred or so students while most public high schools that draw students from many districts have a thousand or more. Another difference is the teachers. High school teachers expect the majority of their students to be independent learners who can turn in quality work. Middle school teachers often allow students a bit more leeway and are more available to give help. They often allow students to revise their work until it meets certain standards. Finally, grades are another area where the two schools differ. In middle school students are urged to do well, but college acceptance does not hinge on middle school grades. However, in high school, grades really count because they determine whether or not students will get into the colleges of their choice! All in all, middle school and high school are two different worlds.

Notice how high school and middle school are compared in the following.

EXAMPLE OF COMPARISON TEXT STRUCTURE

Common Ground

While many students feel that middle school and high school are very different, I feel that they really have a lot in common. First, both have students who must attend classes and meet certain requirements in order to eventually graduate. These students, no matter which school they attend, usually go to school for about the same length of time each year. Next, both schools offer choices of classes, various kinds of clubs, and many athletic programs. Social activities are available to both middle and high schoolers. In both these settings, students mingle together in the hall, stop and chat at their lockers, and join in long conversations over lunch or snacks in the cafeteria for at least forty-five minutes every day. While middle schools and high schools may appear different to some, I think they are really a lot alike.

Note: For a graphic organizer that students can use when they write comparison/contrast pieces see Teacher Tips at the end of chapter 2 (Figure 2.6).

Cause/Effect Text Structure

Consider the following questions as you read.

What is it that happens?

What causes it to happen?

What are the important elements or facts that cause this effect?

How do these factors or elements interrelate?

Will this result always happen from these causes? Why or why not?

How would the result change if the elements or factors were different?

Cause/Effect Text Structure Questions from *Classroom Strategies for Interactive Learning* by Doug Buehl (1995), Wisconsin State Reading Association. Reprinted with permission of the Wisconsin State Reading Association.

Following is an example of cause/effect text structure.

EXAMPLE OF CAUSE/EFFECT TEXT STRUCTURE

Traffic Alert

Hallways can provide many problems for new, inexperienced high school students or transfer students. First, most high school hallways are dark and narrow with heavy hall traffic. Therefore, much congestion occurs during passing periods. This congestion can cause students to drop their books, fall, or even run into other students, which could trigger a shoving match or even a fight! But, that is a minor problem compared to what happens when the hallway ends in a stairwell. Now the congestion problem is compounded as students try to push their way down the stairs. In addition to an accident happening, students often face the ultimate problem: being late for class because they could not get down the stairs, through the next crowded hallway, and into their respective classrooms. While dropping books, falling, or fighting are all big problems, they pale in comparison to a Tardy Detention, given after several late arrivals. Unfortunately, sometimes there is no easy way to avoid being late to class!

Note: For a graphic organizer students can use when they write cause/effect pieces, see Teacher Tips at the end of chapter 2 (Figure 2.5).

Problem/Solution Text Structure

Consider the following questions as you read.

What is the problem?

Who has the problem?

What is causing the problem?

What are the effects of the problem?

Who is trying to solve the problem?

What solutions are recommended or attempted?

What results from these solutions?

Is the problem solved? Do any complications develop because of the solutions?

Problem/Solution Text Structure Questions from *Classroom Strategies for Interactive Learning* by Doug Buehl (1995), Wisconsin State Reading Association. Reprinted with permission of the Wisconsin State Reading Association.

See how a writer handles problem/solution text structure in the following.

EXAMPLE OF PROBLEM/SOLUTION TEXT STRUCTURE

A Daily Dilemma

Tina is having a problem. She is a freshman in high school, and she does not know how she is going to make it to class on time because she is stuck with a locker right by the main entrance, which is a long, long distance from all of the rest of her classes. Because she is a very bright teen, however, she quickly realizes that she can't possibly visit her locker after every class. What, then, will she do? Well, she really has three options. First, she can opt to carry **all** of her books for **all** of her classes around with her **all** day long. But, that is not very appealing. She doesn't want to look like a freshman, which she surely will if she drags every single book and paper around with her. Another option is to find some friends who have lockers close to her classes and store the appropriate books for those classes in their lockers. But, this may not work either since she will have to store her belongings in a locker whose combination is known to at least one other person and maybe even more! That does not make for a very safe situation for storing valuable textbooks and even more valuable homework assignments. So, Tina seizes on the last option: she will carry all the possessions she needs for her morning classes with her and then visit her locker at lunch when she has more time. During that visit, she will gather all her afternoon possessions and finish the day carrying them. While this may not be Tina's ideal plan of action, it will work, and it will prevent her from receiving a dreaded Tardy Detention!

GRAPHIC LITERACY

Implementing specific strategies enables students to read and write in content area subjects; however, for maximum effectiveness, students also need to be able to interpret graphs, tables, and maps—all forms of graphic literacy. Fry (1981) defines graphic literacy as the ability to read, comprehend, and draw five major types of graphs (linear, quantitative, spatial, pictorial, and hypothetical).

Furthermore, visual aids have a specific function. In general, they summarize and condense the written information in a text and communicate the meaning in a visual form. These visual aids, designed to enhance, explain, or clarify concepts or ideas that are written in textbooks, newspapers, and magazines, facilitate understanding the meaning of written material. Most visual aids are directional, so the reader needs to be able to identify key information, interpret and draw inferences from the data, and understand the way the information connects to the text (Vacca and Vacca 1996). Teachers can help students understand the graphics by creating questions or activities that relate to the graphics.

Graphs

A graph is a drawing that shows a relationship between two or more variables of one thing. There are several different kinds of pictorial representations.

1. **Vertical:** The time line is a vertical graph that is numbered and written in order from the beginning of an event to the end. For example, a person's life contributions can be listed chronologically. This graph may be read from right to left or left to right depending on the purpose.

2. **Linear:** This graph is plotted vertically and horizontally and pictures the relationships between two or more variables. For example, a graph might list and give percentages of items students and their parents buy in an office supply store.

3. **Circle:** This graph shows the relationship of parts to the whole. The circle can be divided into sections that can be compared to each other or to the whole. For example, a graph might illustrate the amount of money that families allocate for different items in their budgets.

Tables

A table is an organized display of factual information, usually numbers or statistics. It is frequently arranged in columns or rows. A class schedule is one example of a table.

Maps

A map is a systematic representation of all or part of the Earth on a flat surface. There are certain basic features common to all maps, including a grid (the network of longitude and latitude), a scale, base data (shorelines), a legend or key, and various conventional symbols (e.g., dots for a specified number of people). A map usually has a directional symbol, called a pointer, that indicates the directions of north, south, east, and west on the map.

. . . And this one shows my test anxiety levels.

Graphic Information Lesson

Getting students to interpret and understand graphics in content area textbooks can be a difficult task. Moreover, in order to be effective, students must be able to make connections between the graphic aid, the text, and their prior knowledge. One strategy that works to familiarize students with graphic aids is the Graphic Information Lesson (Reinking 1986). This strategy has three steps in the process.

Stage I

After students have read the text, the teacher carefully goes over a graph, map, or chart with the students, addressing the questions of what information the graphic aid represents and how it pertains to the information found in the text. During this discussion process, students often focus on the literal information found in the graphic aid, but the teacher must model asking higher level inferential and applied questions that show the relationship between the graphic and the part of the text relevant to the graphic. During this process, the teacher also helps students focus on the importance of the graph: Is it redundant, complementary, or supplemental to the text? Figure 1.4 illustrates an effective way to help students understand this stage.

Analyzing a Climograph

Study the graph in Figure 1.4 and answer the following questions. Be sure to note whether you used the graph or textbook information to locate your answers by marking G for graph or T for text before your write each answer.

1. Name the two months when Boston averages below freezing temperatures.
2. In which months might the precipitation come in the form of snow?
3. What is the warmest month in Boston?
4. Does Boston have a dry season? Explain why or why not.
5. Which business would you rather own in Boston, air conditioning or heating? Explain why.
6. When would most crops be planted?
7. Would grapefruits and oranges be grown in this city? Explain why or why not.
8. Would you expect to find a seasonal change of clothing?
9. If seasonal clothing is needed, what kinds of different clothing will be needed?
10. Would you expect to find skiing near Boston?
11. Would you expect to find ice skating near Boston?
12. Would you play hockey indoors or outdoors?
13. Would it be common to find outdoor swimming pools? Why or why not?
14. Would roofs on the houses be flat or pitched? Explain your choice.
15. Add all of the month's average precipitation; what would be Boston's average yearly rainfall in inches? What is its average monthly rainfall?

Stage II

During the second stage, the teacher creates pseudographics or graphic aids that are related to but not presented in the text. They can be consistent or inconsistent with textual information, and they do not have to be accurate, but they do need to be believable or unbelievable, when compared to the text the students have read. Students are asked to survey these pseudographics to determine whether they are believable or unbelievable based on text information and their own prior knowledge, making sure to list page numbers to support their decisions. The focus of this stage is to synthesize the information read and use it to evaluate the graphic aids.

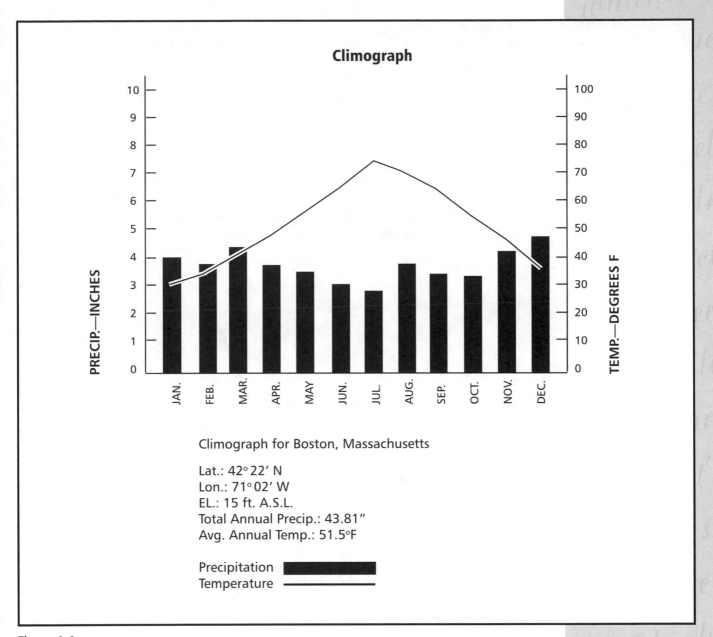

Climograph

Climograph for Boston, Massachusetts

Lat.: 42° 22′ N
Lon.: 71° 02′ W
EL.: 15 ft. A.S.L.
Total Annual Precip.: 43.81″
Avg. Annual Temp.: 51.5°F

Precipitation
Temperature

Figure 1.4

Stage III

In this final stage, students are asked to apply what they have learned about graphic aids and how they are related to the text by actually developing their own pseudographics or evaluating those that are used in the text.

Figures l.5a and l.5b are examples of pseudographics.

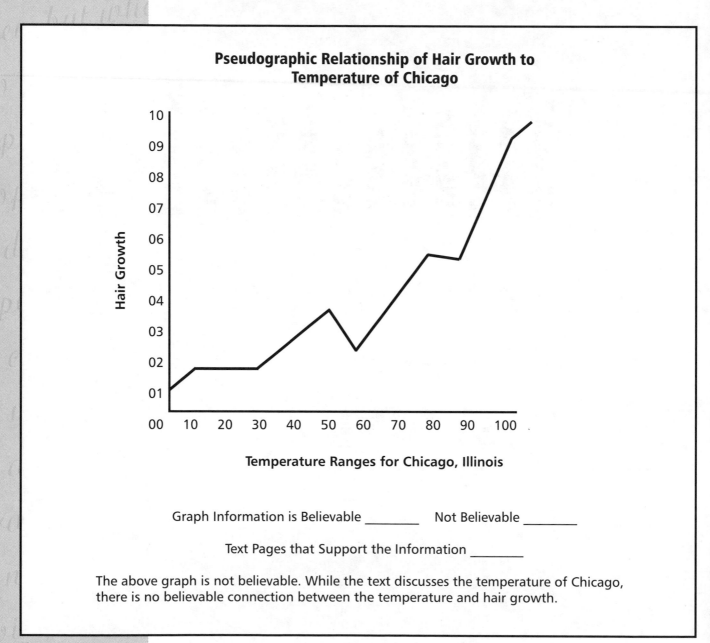

Pseudographic Relationship of Hair Growth to Temperature of Chicago

Temperature Ranges for Chicago, Illinois

Graph Information is Believable _____ Not Believable _____

Text Pages that Support the Information _____

The above graph is not believable. While the text discusses the temperature of Chicago, there is no believable connection between the temperature and hair growth.

Figure 1.5a

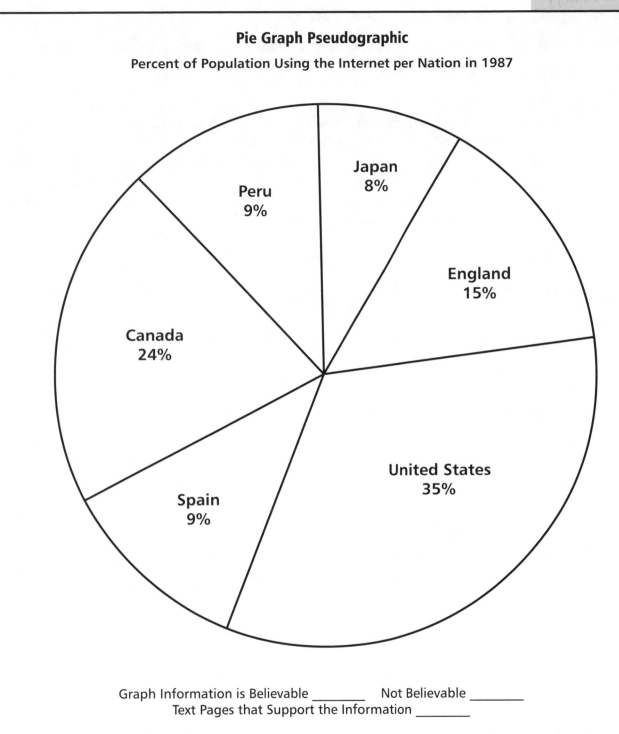

Pie Graph Pseudographic

Percent of Population Using the Internet per Nation in 1987

Japan
8%

Peru
9%

England
15%

Canada
24%

United States
35%

Spain
9%

Graph Information is Believable _____ Not Believable _____
Text Pages that Support the Information _____

The above pseudograph is not believable. While the text discusses the innovation and progression of the Internet, the facts pictured are faulty. In 1987 the Internet was not accessible to all the nations listed. Furthermore, Japan is a more technologically advanced country than Peru, which lacks electricity in vast areas, so the percentage shown is clearly unbelievable.

Figure 1.5b

CHAPTER SUMMARY

Chapter 1 discusses the importance of matching the reader with the text to be read and suggests different methods to assess students' ability to do this. Two specific strategies, the Question-Answer Relationship Strategy (QARS) and the Content Area Reading Inventory (CARI), help students interpret their texts. The chapter also presents five patterns of text structure: (1) definition/example; (2) proposition/support; (3) comparison/contrast; (4) cause/effect; and (5) problem/solution. Students need to identify these five patterns in order to comprehend content area textbooks effectively. Finally, graphic literacy skills enable students to interpret graphs, tables, maps, and other visuals.

COMPUTER CONNECTIONS

1. As a review procedure, place students in groups of five and assign them a section of the chapter to be read. After reading the section, have students draw lots to choose one of the five types of paragraph patterns discussed in the chapter and, using the computer, compose a paragraph highlighting the important points of the section using the pattern of organization they drew. Students then read their paragraphs to the group (or the entire class) and challenge their classmates to identify the pattern of organization used.

2. Place students in groups and assign a different section of the chapter to each group. When the groups have completed reading their assigned sections, have them create three to five questions based on the reading for each of the four QARS types on the computer. Create a file of these questions so that students may use them as a review or you can use them as a form of assessment.

Teacher Tips

❶ Use the following Blackline Master Readability Checklist, Figure 1.6, to rate your textbook.

❷ Use the Raygor Readability Graph, Figure 1.7, to determine the readability of your text.

Directions: Choose three 100-word passages, one at the beginning, one in the middle, and one at the end of the textbook. In the count, include proper nouns, but do not include numbers. Then follow these steps:

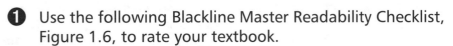

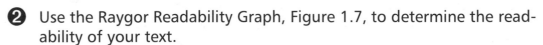

a. Count the number of sentences in each passage, estimating to the nearest tenth.

b. Count the words that have six or more letters.

c. Average the sentence length and the word length over three samples. Then plot the average on the graph.

Readability Checklist

This checklist is designed to help you evaluate the readability of your classroom texts. It can best be used if you rate your text while you are thinking of a specific class. Be sure to compare the textbook to a fictional ideal rather than to another text. Your goal is to find out what aspects of the text are or are not less than ideal. Finally, consider supplementary workbooks as part of the textbook and rate them together. Have fun!

Rate the questions below using the following rating system.
5 = Excellent
4 = Good
3 = Adequate
2 = Poor
1 = Unacceptable
NA = Not Applicable

Further comments may be written in the space provided.

Textbook Title:
Publisher:
Copyright Date:

Understandability

A. _____ Are the assumptions about students' vocabulary knowledge appropriate?
B. _____ Are the assumptions about students' prior knowledge of this content area appropriate?
C. _____ Are the assumptions about students' general experiential backgrounds appropriate?
D. _____ Does the teacher's manual provide the teacher with ways to develop and review the students' conceptual and experiential backgrounds?
E. _____ Are new concepts explicitly linked to the students' prior knowledge or to their experiential backgrounds?
F. _____ Does the text introduce abstract concepts by accompanying them with many concrete examples?
G. _____ Does the text introduce new concepts one at a time with a sufficient number of examples for each one?
H. _____ Are definitions understandable and at a lower level of abstraction than the concept being claimed?
I. _____ Is the level of sentence complexity appropriate for the students?
J. _____ Are the main ideas of paragraphs, chapters, and subsections clearly stated?
K. _____ Does the text avoid irrelevant details?
L. _____ Does the text explicitly state important complex relationships (e.g., causality, conditionality, etc.) rather than always expecting the reader to infer them from the context?
M. _____ Does the teacher's manual provide lists of accessible resources containing alternative readings for the very poor or very advanced readers?
N. _____ Is the readability level appropriate (according to a readability formula)?

(continued on next page)

Figure 1.6

SkyLight Professional Development

Learnability

Organization

A. _____ Is an introduction provided in each chapter?

B. _____ Is there a clear and simple organizational pattern relating the chapters to each other?

C. _____ Does each chapter have a clear, explicit, and simple organizational structure?

D. _____ Does the text include resources such as an index, glossary, and table of contents?

E. _____ Do questions and activities draw attention to the organizational pattern of the material (e.g., chronological, cause and effect, spatial, topical, etc.)?

F. _____ Do consumable materials interrelate well with the textbook?

Reinforcement

A. _____ Does the text provide opportunities for students to practice concepts?

B. _____ Are there summaries at appropriate intervals in the text?

C. _____ Does the text provide adequate iconic aids such as maps, graphs, illustrations, etc. to reinforce concepts?

D. _____ Are there adequate suggestions for usable supplementary activities?

E. _____ Do these activities provide for a broad range of ability levels?

F. _____ Are there literal recall questions provided for the students' self-review?

G. _____ Do some of the questions encourage the students to draw inferences?

H. _____ Are there discussion questions which encourage creative thinking?

I. _____ Are questions clearly worded?

Motivation

A. _____ Does the teacher's manual provide introductory activities that will capture the students' interests?

B. _____ Are chapter titles and subheadings concrete, meaningful, or interesting?

C. _____ Is the writing style of the text appealing to the students?

D. _____ Are the activities motivating? Will they make the student want to pursue the topic further?

E. _____ Does the book clearly show how the knowledge being learned might be used by the learner in the future?

F. _____ Are the cover, format, print size, and pictures appealing to the students?

G. _____ Does the text provide positive and motivating models for both sexes as well as for other racial, ethnic, and socioeconomic groups?

Readability Analysis

Weaknesses

1. On which items was the book rated the lowest?
2. Did these items tend to fall into certain categories?
3. Summarize the weaknesses of this text.
4. What can you do in class to compensate for the weaknesses of this text?

Assets

1. On which items was the book rated the highest?
2. Did these items fall in certain categories?
3. Summarize the assets of this text.
4. What can you do in class to take advantage of the assets of this text?

Checklist from Irwin, J. W. and Davis, C. A. (1980, November). Assessing readability: The checklist approach. *The Journal of Reading*, *24*(2), 129–130. Reprinted with permission of Judith W. Irwin and the International Reading Association. All rights reserved.

Figure 1.6 (continued)

Raygor Readability Graph

Choose three 100-word passages, one at the beginning, one in the middle, and one at the end of the textbook. In the count, include proper nouns, but do not include numbers. Then follow these steps:

a. Count the number of sentences in each passage, estimating to the nearest tenth.

b. Count the words that have six or more letters.

c. Average the sentence length and the word length over three samples. Then plot the average on the graph.

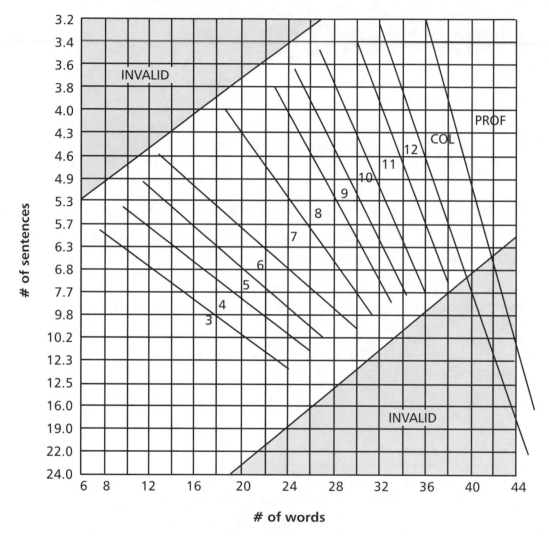

Worksheet:

	Sentences	Number of Words
Sample A	_____	_____
Sample B	_____	_____
Sample C	_____	_____
TOTAL	_____	_____
AVERAGE	_____	_____

Figure 1.7

Setting the Framework for Writing

Writing is thinking. It is more than living, for it is being conscious of living.

Anne Morrow Lindbergh

THE WRITING PROCESS

CREATING
- Looping
- Clustering
- Immersion (Process Writing*)

TERMS FOR WRITING
- Audience
- Lead
- Thesis
- Support
- Transitions
- Conclusion

SHAPING ORGANIZATIONAL APPROACHES
- Chronological Order (Process Writing: Narrative and Process/How-To*)
- Spatial Order
- General to Specific Order (Cause/Effect and Comparison/Contrast)*
- Specific to General Order (Cause/Effect and Comparison/Contrast)*
- Emphatic Order

SHAPING AND DRAFTING THE CONTENT

REVISING THE ESSAY

CHAPTER SUMMARY

*Indicates that a Blackline Master is included in Teacher Tips at the end of the chapter.

THE WRITING PROCESS

Imagine a child who is learning how to ride a bike. A parent may put him on the bike, push him, run behind him, and even hold onto the fender. But as soon as the parent lets go, the child might fall off. It takes a lot of practice for a child to feel confident about riding off on his own.

Like a child learning to ride a bike, we all need practice to master any skill, particularly writing. Since every written piece is different, it requires a different approach and some thought. Writing is an attempt to transform our ideas into words. As Anne Morrow Lindbergh tells us, "Writing is thinking." Therefore, if we want students to become better writers, we need to provide some opportunities to practice the craft of writing. Usually we learn any craft by proceeding in steps. Although there are multiple approaches to help students write effectively, certain approaches are more manageable than others. The writing process model used in classrooms now provides opportunities for students to learn the stages of writing. A familiar model of the writing process model includes these terms: prewriting, drafting, and revision. We chose to use the terms *creating*, *shaping*, and *revising* for our process model.

CREATING

The term *creating* implies generating and forming ideas. In this stage of the process, students practice prewriting techniques as well as other strategies to help them master the skill of writing. The prewriting stage is the most important part of the process. In this phase, students can gather their thoughts before they begin to write, explore topics, experiment with style and form, and record their ideas without worrying about a grade. Thus, teachers need to design a variety of activities to help students approach a piece of writing.

Brainstorming is an effective way to generate topics for any writing assignment. Before every assignment, our students generate a list of topics, and we record them on the blackboard. This strategy stimulates their memories and gives them ideas for writing. As a follow-up activity, we frequently ask students to choose one of the topics and do a free focus write (Zemelman and Daniels 1988). Students write continuously for a given period of time, usually six to ten minutes nonstop, and focus on the topic without worrying about the correct form or grammar. Then we ask them to share their writing with a partner, a small group, or with the whole class. This strategy not only fosters thinking; it helps students explore topics and evaluate classmates' work without fear. There are several other prewriting strategies that are useful and help provide variety. Three strategies that are particularly effective in our classrooms are *looping*, *clustering*, and *immersion*.

Looping

Have students choose one of the generated topics. Instruct them to write for three to five minutes and then stop. Tell them to read through the writing and circle key words or phrases in that passage. Next, have them write again, focusing on the circled words or phrases. Encourage them to repeat the procedure and write again. Students now have a sequence of free writings, each more specific than the first one. This strategy provides a graphic organizer that highlights the key words and/or phrases. It also helps students develop details related to a topic and promotes the use of the verbal/linguistic, logical/mathematical, visual/spatial, and intrapersonal intelligences. For a full explanation of all the multiple intelligences, see the section on the immersion strategy.

Clustering

Clustering is a form of mapping that explores the relationship between words. The writer chooses a topic and writes it in a circle in the middle of a page. As associated ideas come, the writer arranges the words or phrases around the first word, circling them and drawing lines to show the connections (Zemelman and Daniels 1988). The result looks like a web on the page. It is easy for students to distinguish how the ideas fit together and to visualize the possible directions the paper might take. This strategy promotes critical thinking, idea building, and organizational skills. It also promotes the verbal/linguistic, logical/mathematical, visual/spatial, and intrapersonal intelligences.

Immersion

As teachers, we are aware that our students do not have the same interests and abilities and do not learn in the same way. However, all students have the potential to learn skills and develop their unique abilities. Writers need to have the capability to use different patterns of development (e.g., process, comparison and contrast) to describe and organize their ideas. Because each pattern has its own distinct logic, students need to understand how each one works. If we explain how each of the patterns is connected to real-life experiences either by immersing students in a real-life experience or simulating one in the classroom, students will be more likely to understand them (Fogarty 1997).

Immersion is the practice of using Gardner's multiple intelligences theory (1983) to focus on a pattern of writing development. Psychologist Howard Gardner has identified eight intelligences: verbal/linguistic, logical/ mathematical, visual/ spatial, bodily/kinesthetic, musical/rhythmic, intrapersonal, and interpersonal, adding the naturalist intelligence in

1995. The teacher chooses the pattern of development and models how it works by giving examples in the chosen multiple intelligences. Sharon Thiese designed a specific immersion strategy of this nature to help students recognize each pattern of writing by connecting these patterns to the multiple intelligences and by using examples that are familiar to students' lives. Notice how the immersion strategy works with seven of the multiple intelligences in the example of a process essay.

PROCESS ESSAY

1. Verbal/Linguistic

The teacher gives directions for each of the examples below for students to follow.

2. Intrapersonal

a. Have each student write a definition of a process.

b. Record answers on the board.

c. Next, ask students to give examples.

Logical/Mathematical

a. Give directions from Geneva High School (Logan Avenue) to Starbucks™.

b. Explain the procedure for buying a lunch in the cafeteria.

Bodily/Kinesthetic

a. Act out or write out how to swing on a swing.

b. Act out or write out how to shoot a basket.

Musical/Rhythmic

Listen to the recording and indicate how many times you hear a change in the melody. (The overture from *Oklahoma* is an effective choice of music.)

Interpersonal

The class generates a list of possible topics. Some examples include how to play a sport, how to write a business letter, how to procrastinate, how to have the perfect date, how animals survive in the wilderness, or how moviemakers create special effects.

Visual/Spatial

Students use a graphic organizer to record their ideas before they write the rough draft. See Figure 2.1 for a sample graphic organizer. For a Blackline Master that your students can use to plan their process papers, see Teacher Tips at the end of this chapter (Figure 2.4).

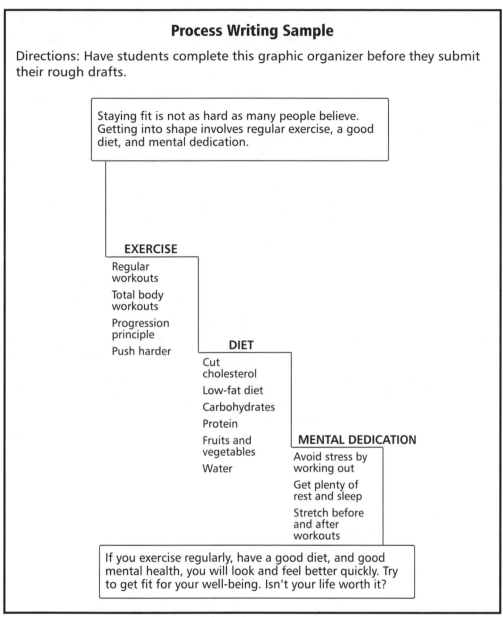

Process Writing Sample

Directions: Have students complete this graphic organizer before they submit their rough drafts.

Staying fit is not as hard as many people believe. Getting into shape involves regular exercise, a good diet, and mental dedication.

EXERCISE

Regular workouts

Total body workouts

Progression principle

Push harder

DIET

Cut cholesterol

Low-fat diet

Carbohydrates

Protein

Fruits and vegetables

Water

MENTAL DEDICATION

Avoid stress by working out

Get plenty of rest and sleep

Stretch before and after workouts

If you exercise regularly, have a good diet, and good mental health, you will look and feel better quickly. Try to get fit for your well-being. Isn't your life worth it?

Figure 2.1

Terms for Writing

Giving students the opportunity to practice different forms of prewriting is only one part in the process of creating. Encouraging students to practice different forms and styles of writing, without grading them, will set a climate for learning. In fact, practice is an important part of mastering any skill, particularly vocabulary. Just as artists need to be familiar with terms like *gesso*, *easel*, and *pallet* to understand the tools for developing their craft, writers also need to know the terms that will help them perfect

Please say you'll accept this as my rough draft.

the craft of writing. Teachers need to design activities to familiarize students with six essential terms for writing: *audience, lead, thesis, support, transitions,* and *conclusion.* Giving students the opportunity to become familiar with each term will facilitate learning. Students will not only recognize the term but, with practice, will be able to understand how it is related to writing and will be able to apply it to their own writing.

Audience

Writing does not exist in isolation; it grows out of experience. Whatever your purpose for writing, your written words will be read by teachers, friends, parents, and others. These readers are your audience. Audience is not merely a matter of just any people; the people in your audience exist in a particular place and time and have their own beliefs and customs. Before you write, you must decide how you will address your readers. Certainly, a teen who is unhappy with her job would complain to her friends, her parents, and her boss each in a different way. Similarly, sensitivity to your audience's interests and needs will make a difference in the way you approach your topic and communicate with your readers.

 Steps for Identifying Audience

1. Think about your topic, the purpose of your paper, and your viewpoint.
2. Define your audience by asking questions:
   a. Who needs to know this information? Males? Females? A combined audience?
   b. What is the age group of my readers? Are they adults, teens, or children?
   c. What formed opinions and values do readers have?
   d. What are the interests and needs of these readers?
   e. How can I relate to the readers?
3. Anticipate the readers' responses to your ideas, and choose words and a style of writing that will relate to their interests and needs.

In order to help students understand the importance of communicating to a specific audience, teachers should let their students practice. They should choose one topic and create different assignments that target specific audiences. Small groups of students can complete the assignments and share them with the class.

In the following examples, notice how audience determines the writer's handling of the subject matter.

YOUR AUDIENCE DETERMINES HOW YOU HANDLE A TOPIC

Notice how writers handle the topic of nutrition differently depending on the interests, ages, and needs of their particular audiences.

A. Writer: a student in a biology class

Assignment: define *nutrition*

Audience: a biology or health teacher

Nutrition is the study of foods and their compositions and the ways the chemical components are made available to the body for its growth and maintenance. The adequacy of the food supply and the mechanisms that transfer the food supply to the body's tissues determine a person's nutritive state.

B. Writer: a student in an English class

Assignment: write a persuasive essay

Audience: fellow students

What is the number one food choice among teens today? Pizza, of course. While it provides some nutritional value, the fat content is quite high. By simply choosing more low-fat foods, teens can have a healthier lifestyle.

C. Writer: a member of the student council who buys lunch in the cafeteria

Assignment: write a request

Audience: cafeteria managers

The members of the student council would like your help. The menu that we currently have in our cafeteria is very limited. In fact, we get hamburgers, fries, and pizza every day. Since many students are trying to eat a well-balanced meal or are vegetarians, we would like to meet with you so we can plan a menu that will provide a variety of options for the student body. We are available to meet with you during any of the lunch hours next week.

D. Writer: a student who is having a birthday

Assignment: explain what you want to have at a party

Audience: parents

Mom and Dad,

Thanks for letting me plan my own birthday party. We don't need to have any fancy paper plates or decorations; balloons will be fine. I'd like to have the party Saturday afternoon at 5. I'll make my own invitations and mail them for you.

I think it would be fun to cook hamburgers and hot dogs on the grill. We can also serve chips, pretzels, and soda. I'd like to have chocolate cake since it's my favorite.

Lead

Professional writers know the importance of getting the reader's attention in the beginning of a piece of writing. Without an effective lead, the reader can lose interest and quit reading. The lead is found in the introductory paragraph that leads or guides the reader into the writer's thoughts and ideas. The lead establishes the authority of the writer speaking to the reader and promises to satisfy the reader's expectations (Murray 1985). The lead needs to arouse the reader's interest, introduce the subject, and establish the focus and direction for the paper.

 Steps for Writing a Lead

1. Examine your ideas to discover the central issue in the subject.
2. Determine the purpose and direction of the writing.
3. Try different types of leads to see what works best with the piece of writing.

In order to help students understand how a lead can change the slant of a paper, teachers can assign one topic and ask small groups of students to write three different leads and then share their examples with the class. The authors model this strategy in the following examples by using the topic of food in the first example of each type of lead.

Notice how you can capture your readers' attention immediately with an effective lead.

EXAMPLES OF LEADS

Give Background Information about the Topic

The writer gives the reader a specific bit of information that will reveal necessary details about a particular person, place, and/or event that will inform, interest, and intrigue the reader.

> The earliest form of pizza was a crude bread that was baked beneath the stones of the fire. After cooking, it was seasoned with a variety of toppings and used instead of plates and utensils to sop up broth and gravies. Legend tells us that this idea came from the Greeks who ate flat round bread (*plankuntos*) baked with an assortment of toppings. They ate it because it was a thrifty and convenient food.

The writer provides information about the education in Colonial America in the following example using background information.

> Children who attended school in colonial times experienced a different setting from students today. Students of all ages were crowded into a small room,

frequently heated by a fire. They had very few books and were often required to repeat their lessons until they memorized them. The Bible was essential reading material for everyone. Teachers believed in strict punishment for students who didn't follow the rules.

Anecdote

The writer tells a brief story in order to involve the reader in the story and to reveal the essence of the piece of writing.

Every night at dinner, it was the same old thing. My Dad had this strange idea that we needed to take a portion of everything my Mom served and eat it. He made us sit at the table until our plates were clean. After several nights of sitting at the table for two or more hours, I decided to take things into my own hands and devise some different ways to dispose of the foods I hated to eat.

The next writer uses a different anecdote to describe a somewhat frightening, eye-opening experience at school.

I remember the day I entered my new school. I pushed my way through a crowd of students who stood in groups blocking my way. One crowd of boys kicked a tennis ball back and forth across the tile floor. I dodged the ball and passed another group who leaned against the wall chewing candy bars and tossing the wrappers on the floor. Their shouts echoed through the dimly lit building as I tried to find my way to my first hour class. I stood in front of the broken door and realized that just getting through the day would be a challenge. Would I make it?

Quotation

A quotation from a familiar source captures the reader's attention, has a ring of authority, and often states a universal truth. Daily newspapers and news magazines are good sources for finding quotations for current topics. *Bartlett's Familiar Quotations* provides examples of a more general nature. Choose a quote that illustrates the significance of the piece of writing.

Remember students, when you're planning your diet, "you are what you eat." So let's take a look at the four food groups and see how to plan for a well-balanced diet!

In the second account that follows, you can see how a familiar quotation enlivens a common situation.

When I was a child, my mother repeatedly said, "Money is the root of all evil." Now that I'm an adult and have overextended my credit limit, I understand the meaning of her words.

Questions

The reader's interest can be stimulated by asking a question or series of questions that do not have an immediate answer and that will engage the reader in finding the answers.

> Is there an easy way to eat more healthful foods? Do any of the new diets work? What about trying vitamins or nutritional supplements? Will exercise help? I need to find the right answer so I can feel better.

Read the excerpt that follows and see how this questioning approach directs your attention to the issue of suitability of many television shows for children.

> Should children be allowed to watch anything that is televised? What if a show contains violence or vulgar language? What if it shows inappropriate dress? These are questions that concern parents today.

Thesis

The thesis is a statement that presents the paper's limited subject and the writer's attitude about that subject. It is generally expressed in one or two sentences and is placed after the lead.

> Staying fit isn't as hard as many people believe. Getting into shape involves regular exercise, a good diet, and mental dedication.

Support

It is almost impossible to understand a general concept without examples. Examples are used in all fields. For instance, a guidance counselor uses test scores as an indicator for course choices, a biologist uses the findings from a recent lab experiment to write a report, and a sports team names their most valuable player because of his or her record. Good writing also needs examples. Without clear and specific examples, writing has no purpose. In practical application, a body paragraph may exhibit two or more methods of support; however, for purposes of explanation, a description of each method follows.

Each body paragraph of the essay should support the thesis statement. A topic sentence, which generally appears at the beginning of the paragraph, states the main idea. Writers can support their views by using **facts, examples of actual events, details about people or places,** and **statistics** that are generally known by the public or are documented in print. For instance, that Springfield is the capital of Illinois, that spinach is a good source of vitamin A, and that Richard Nixon resigned from the presidency in 1974 are facts anyone can confirm. Writers can use facts to explain, inform, and clarify ideas.

Writers can also support their views with **opinions.** While an opinion can be based on facts, usually it is based on what the writer believes to be the case or on the writer's observation. Opinions cannot always be verified.

For instance, that General Patton was a controversial leader, that life exists on other planets, and that vitamin C can prevent a cold are all opinions, not facts. However, writers can make their opinions believable by giving solid evidence to support their views, thus validating the opinion.

Choosing examples that include **illustrations** or **personal anecdotes** is one of the most effective ways to support the topic sentence. The writer describes personal experiences he or she has witnessed, thus making connections to the reader's experiences.

In the writing model that follows, you will notice how the writer effectively blends facts, illustrations, and opinions in a description of a very crowded school.

WRITING MODEL

Note that the sample paragraph includes facts, illustrations, and opinion.

Lincoln High School, which can accommodate 1,500 students, is completely overcrowded. **(fact)** More than 2,000 students enter the building each day. **(fact)** The lack of space is apparent in all parts of the building. The hallways are so packed that students have to push their way through the crowd to get to their classes on time. Every classroom is filled with 30 or more desks and books are piled everywhere. **(illustration)** Every inch of this building is so crammed that it is difficult for students to move. These congested conditions are dangerous and need to be improved to facilitate learning. **(opinion)**

Transitions

Transition words, or signal devices, help readers follow the progression points between paragraphs. Some examples of transition words that can help you link your paragraphs together are as follows:

Example of Transitions

Time	Addition	Contrast
• first	• another	• but
• second	• in addition to	• however
• next	• furthermore	• on the other hand
• then	• also	• unlike

Space	Comparison	Summary
• above	• similarly	• thus
• below	• too	• therefore
• next to	• likewise	• in brief
• under	• in the same way	• finally

Conclusion

Imagine watching a television series and missing the last episode. That would be frustrating. Likewise, a writer who does not provide closure to a piece of writing disappoints the readers. These readers have not had the chance to completely comprehend the writer's ideas. Like the introduction, the conclusion is a necessary part of an essay. It pulls together the main supporting points of discussion, reinforces the thesis, and gives the writer a sense of fulfillment. Since the writer has one last opportunity to state the points of the essay, the conclusion needs to be strong, interesting, and convincing. Most importantly, it must provide closure.

Writers need to practice writing different types of conclusions to determine what works best. Following are several different methods for writing a conclusion.

DIFFERENT TYPES OF CONCLUSIONS

Offer a Solution or Make a Recommendation

Use this technique if the composition describes a problem. Notice how the writer in the Quotation section of the Examples of Leads who began a composition with the quotation "Money is the root of all evil" recommends a solution for managing money in the conclusion.

> I've discovered that it's easier to manage my money by writing out a budget and then following it. I've learned to avoid impulse buying and lending money. Instead, I put money aside for savings. Try these simple steps if you want to avoid spending more than you earn.

Pose a Dramatic Question or Challenge

Look at the way the writer challenges readers to improve their diets. (This conclusion follows the persuasive essay in the Audience section.)

> Think about changing your own eating habits. By choosing food items that contain less salt, less fat, and more fiber, you can look better and feel better in a few weeks. It is worth giving up a bag of potato chips to have a healthier lifestyle.

Bring the Reader Full Circle

By referring back to the lead, the writer connects his ideas to the background information about Colonial America. (This conclusion follows the Background Information in the Examples of Leads section.)

> The classroom atmosphere has improved dramatically since colonial times. We have electricity, a variety of books, and materials that are student-friendly. Teachers and students now have the opportunity to work together to provide a better learning environment for all.

SHAPING ORGANIZATIONAL PATTERNS

Did you ever try to clean out a junk drawer or try to decide what items to put in a garage sale? Both of these processes require some thought and organizational skills. Likewise, students have to make decisions about which parts of the creating process they will use to shape their ideas to effectively communicate to the reader. Students need to determine whether they are writing a single paragraph, multiple paragraphs, or an entire essay. Part of the shaping process also includes organization.

Readers look for organization in everything they read. When they read, they determine which ideas are important and how those ideas relate to other ideas that are written. Therefore, writers need to organize their ideas in order to have a clear focus and communicate their points to the reader.

Wait until our teacher sees my illustration of the writing process.

Writers use various patterns of development to develop and organize their ideas. Because each pattern has its own logic, each one encourages the writer to think about a subject in a different way. The writer must always consider the purpose of the paper in order to use the correct pattern or combination of organizational patterns of development.

As a writer, you can select among five general approaches to organizing the evidence in an essay: *chronological, spatial, general to specific, specific to general,* and *emphatic.*

Chronological Order (Narrative and Process/How-to)

Supporting material is arranged in a time sequence, usually starting with what happened first and ending with what happened last. Writers who narrate an event or explain a process usually use the chronological approach throughout the entire paper. It is appropriate to use chronological order in describing a chain of events.

Steps for a Narrative

1. Every narrative presents a span of time and ends at a certain point. Jot down the major details of an event as it happened.
2. Focus on the main event and eliminate any details that do not support it.
3. Organize the narrative sequence in chronological order.
4. Use transitional words such as *before, next, later,* and *after* to signal every change in time, place, or direction.

 ### *Steps for a Process/How-to*

1. Jot down the primary and secondary steps or sequences that are involved in the process.
2. Make sure the details are accurate and in the correct order.
3. Include transitional words such as *first, second, next, then,* and *finally* to signal what happens at each stage of the process and to help the reader understand the order of the steps.

See Teacher Tips at the end of the chapter for a Process Writing Blackline Master (Figure 2.4).

WRITING MODEL

Before you choose a college, it is important to consider the cost. First, set a price range that establishes what you are willing or able to pay for your future education. For example, it might be easier to finance four years at Northern Illinois University, which costs approximately eight thousand dollars a year, over Northwestern University, which costs thirty thousand a year. Next, decide how you will pay for your expenses. While a part-time job might cover essentials, it will not cover all of your expenses. Look into applying for financial aid, obtaining a scholarship, or borrowing the money from your parents or relatives. Then, create a budget that will not only meet your needs, but that will enable you to finish school without going into debt. Remember, if you cannot afford to attend a particular college, you need to look elsewhere.

Spatial Order

Supporting material is arranged according to where things happen or where things are. This strategy is particularly appropriate for description. Generally, the writer's point of vision is explained by the order in which the details are observed and described. Therefore, the writer needs to determine a fixed point of view from which the person, object, or view is observed and described. For example, while describing a person the writer could give the details from head to foot or vice versa. However, when writing about a particular place, the writer might describe the objects in the place from nearest to farthest or vice versa. Using transitional words such as *right to left, top to bottom,* or *in front* or *behind* guide the reader.

 ### Steps for Spatial Order

1. Determine a point of vision.
2. Choose specific details that will give the reader a picture of the person or place.
3. Select the organizational pattern that best supports your point of vision and observation.
4. Use transitional words so that the reader can follow the description.

WRITING MODEL

The students started to assemble their assignment to prepare a bulletin board display that illustrated the features of the Middle Ages. They agreed to arrange the pictures according to the categories they had researched. One boy picked up the pictures relating to the Feudal System and stapled them on the far left corner of the bulletin board. Then he selected the illustrations depicting medieval clothing and placed them next to the first set of pictures. One of the girls handed him the drawings that portrayed men's and women's roles in society, and he stapled them underneath the other pictures. Another girl handed him the illustrations about the entertainment of the time. He placed them on the bottom of the bulletin board. Finally, the last girl picked up the cut out letters that said "Middle Ages" and stapled them across the top of the bulletin board. The students smiled at the display, knowing that their classmates would enjoy it.

General to Specific Order

The purpose of this pattern is to help readers understand the general statement. Supporting materials are arranged to start with a general statement, often a topic sentence, and progress to specific explanations of that statement. The material becomes more specific as the examples develop in the paragraph. This strategy is effective in cause/effect, comparison/contrast, classification, and argumentation essays. See Figure 2.2 for a sample cause/effect graphic organizer. Also see Figure 2.3 for a sample comparison/contrast graphic organizer.

 Steps for General to Specific Order

1. The topic sentence should identify a general statement about the subject.
2. The writer should choose details that make specific points about the general statement.
3. The writer should make sure the reader can understand and relate to the specific examples.

WRITING MODEL

Our growing concern with obtaining a healthier lifestyle has affected the way young people eat. For the last few years, the media has warned us about the dangers of a diet that is too high in salt and fat and too low in fiber. Today, hamburgers and hot dogs may not be the most popular items at your local school cafeteria. Students and their families have started to look for healthier foods, and manufacturers have created new products. The food industry has made items such as lunch meat, cheese, snacks, and soups available in low-fat, low-sodium versions. Grocers have stocked the shelves with multigrain cereals and high-fiber breads. In addition, the food industry has produced all-natural products, such as certain brands of ice cream, without any additives. Finally, healthful fish and salads have become the food of choice, replacing the once favored, but less nutritious, foods.

Specific to General Order

This pattern is an exact reversal of the previous pattern with the specific statement introducing the paragraph and the general statement ending it.

Emphatic Order

When writers use emphatic order, they place the most dramatic item in a series at the end of the paragraph. The order has a built-in momentum because the writer begins with the least important example and builds to the most important ones. This method is particularly effective in argumentation essays and in papers developed through examples such as cause/effect and comparison/contrast essays. See Figures 2.2 and 2.3 for

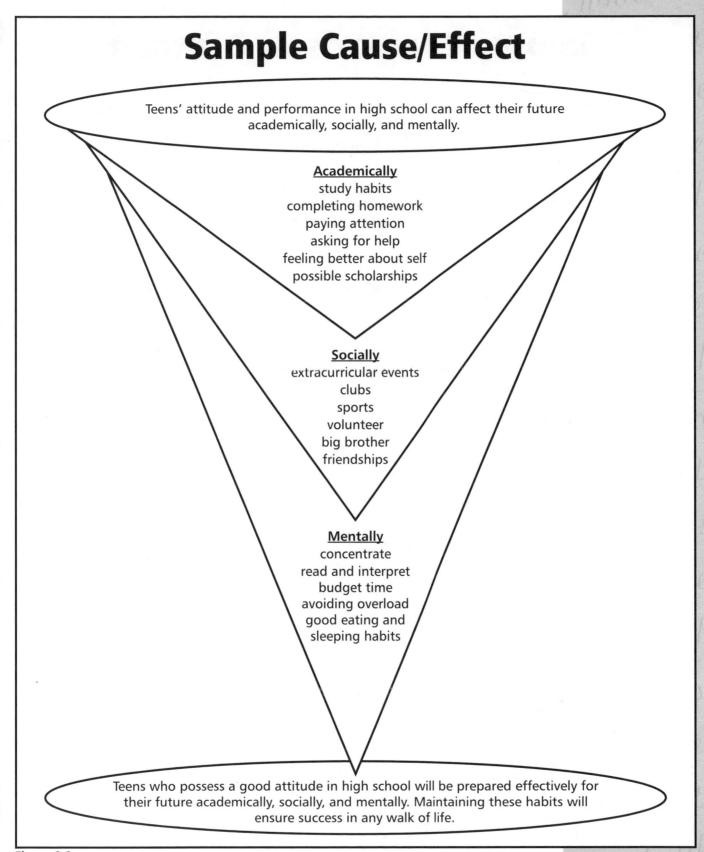

Sample Cause/Effect

Teens' attitude and performance in high school can affect their future
academically, socially, and mentally.

Academically
study habits
completing homework
paying attention
asking for help
feeling better about self
possible scholarships

Socially
extracurricular events
clubs
sports
volunteer
big brother
friendships

Mentally
concentrate
read and interpret
budget time
avoiding overload
good eating and
sleeping habits

Teens who possess a good attitude in high school will be prepared effectively for
their future academically, socially, and mentally. Maintaining these habits will
ensure success in any walk of life.

Figure 2.2

Sample Comparison/Contrast

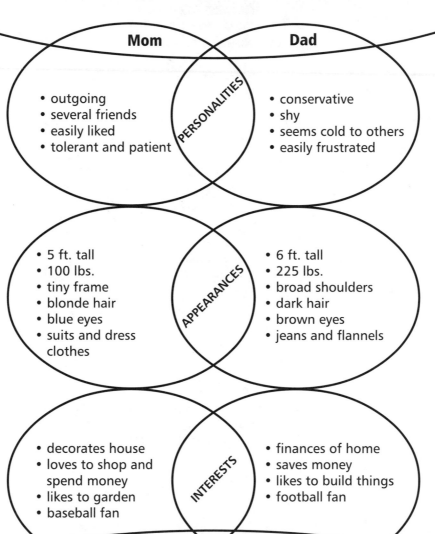

My mom and dad fit the saying "opposites attract." Their personalities, appearances, and interests are different.

Mom   **Dad**

PERSONALITIES

- outgoing
- several friends
- easily liked
- tolerant and patient

- conservative
- shy
- seems cold to others
- easily frustrated

APPEARANCES

- 5 ft. tall
- 100 lbs.
- tiny frame
- blonde hair
- blue eyes
- suits and dress clothes

- 6 ft. tall
- 225 lbs.
- broad shoulders
- dark hair
- brown eyes
- jeans and flannels

INTERESTS

- decorates house
- loves to shop and spend money
- likes to garden
- baseball fan

- finances of home
- saves money
- likes to build things
- football fan

Even though my mom and dad have different personalities, appearances, and interests, it's easy to tell that they really care about each other.

Figure 2.3

SkyLight Professional Development

sample graphic organizers. Also see Teacher Tips at the end of the chapter for Blackline Masters (Figures 2.5 and 2.6).

 ### *Steps for Emphatic Order*

1. Identify an issue and the controversy surrounding it.
2. Provide evidence to support your stance.
3. Arrange the evidence so the most compelling point is last.

Note how the writer lets the reader know the importance of joining extracurricular activities in the example that follows.

WRITING MODEL

An increasing number of schools provide an activity night for students. The purpose of this event is to let students know about the extracurricular activities that are available in their school. It also gives them the opportunity to talk to other students and learn about the purpose of each activity. In addition, coaches and club advisors are available to talk with students about the time commitment that is involved for each activity and to explain the benefits of joining. In fact, they will tell students that an increasing number of colleges look at students' extracurricular activities as part of the admissions process. College admissions officers know that students who can maintain good grades and be involved in extracurricular activities at the same time will be more successful.

SHAPING AND DRAFTING THE CONTENT

Knowing different ways to order information (such as chronological, spatial, general to specific, specific to general, and emphatic) will certainly help in arranging the evidence in an essay, but there are other ways to manage the content of writing an essay. These are frequently called *patterns of organization* or *rhetorical approaches*. They are really ways of structuring information to shape the reader's understanding. Included among these strategies are: *comparison/contrast, process, cause/effect, definition, argumentation,* and *classification*.

NOTE: If you assign comparison/contrast, cause/effect, or process papers to your students, you can use the blackline masters for these strategies offered in Teacher Tips at the end of this chapter (Figures 2.4, 2.5, and 2.6).

These organizational patterns are used every day. For example, when a person buys a pair of running shoes, she goes through the process of deciding which brands she wants to try. She then narrows her choices down to one brand (or classification) and may compare several styles before she makes a purchase. If she makes her choice on how well the shoes will wear on her long morning run, she then incorporates cause and effect into her decision making process.

There is often a gap between the way a person thinks about accomplishing a task and the way a writer composes an essay. When students write, they need to communicate their ideas to a reader who cannot directly question the writer's logic. Therefore, writers need to consider the organizational patterns and determine which ones fit the purpose of the essay so the reader can follow their thinking. Each pattern of development has its own internal logic that makes it appropriate for some writing purposes but not for others. Once writers determine which pattern (or combination of patterns) is implied in their purpose, they can plan the general structure of the essay and write a first draft.

Writing a first draft is a process of discovery involving the continual exploration, clarification, and refining of ideas. In this draft, writers jot down all of their ideas about the topic until they are finished. Once writers complete this process, they have something tangible to read and revise. They do not need to worry about perfect grammar at this stage of the process.

REVISING THE ESSAY

Revision, according to Murray (1985), is not just one step in the writing process, but a series of steps that may need to be frequently repeated. If we expect our students to become better writers, we need to provide some strategies that will help them revise. Teachers might consider using some of the following ideas:

1. Encourage students to read their drafts aloud. It helps students to hear the way a piece sounds, and it makes it easier to detect problems in style or grammar.

2. Have students write a reflection on each draft of their writing, setting goals for improvement.

3. Create a checklist to help students look for ways to improve their writing. We frequently ask them to use the same criteria that we will use in grading their essays.

4. Provide a peer editing sheet for each essay and ask students to have two other people read their work and write suggestions for improvement on the peer editing sheet.

5. Students need to listen to their readers and make changes as needed. You might ask students to respond to their readers.

6. Advise students to revise in steps. They should first look at overall meaning and content; next, at sentence and paragraph development; finally, at grammar.

All writing takes time, thought, and practice. Writers can improve the quality of their work if they remember to use the writing process.

CHAPTER SUMMARY

Chapter 2 emphasizes the importance of giving students practice in all phases of the writing process. By clearly defining and describing each phase of writing, students can grasp each stage separately and build on the process. Providing strategies for creating, shaping, and revising their work also gives students the confidence and the tools they need to master writing.

COMPUTER CONNECTIONS

1. As a review procedure, place students in two teams. Have both teams think of a topic and then create three different audiences and three different assignments for that topic. The two teams switch topics, audiences, and assignment selections, and then each team chooses one of the assignments to complete. The assignment is typed using the computer, and completed written pieces are shared with the class. The teacher can print all the assignments out to compile a book of examples for future use or for class review or assessment.

2. As an alternative to the above, students can individually complete the assignments on the computer and e-mail their written essays to a partner for peer editing. After the editing is completed and corrections made, the teacher can print out the essays and compile a class book exhibiting all the student writing.

Teacher Tips

❶ Whenever students brainstorm topics, assign one student to input topic ideas in a "Topics File" using the computer. This will provide a handy list of ready topics for the future use of both the teacher and students.

❷ Distribute copies of the following Blackline Masters of graphic organizers to help your students plan their papers.

a. Process Writing (Figure 2.4)

b. Cause/Effect (Figure 2.5)

c. Comparison/Contrast (Figure 2.6)

Process Writing

Directions: Have students complete this graphic organizer before they submit their rough drafts.

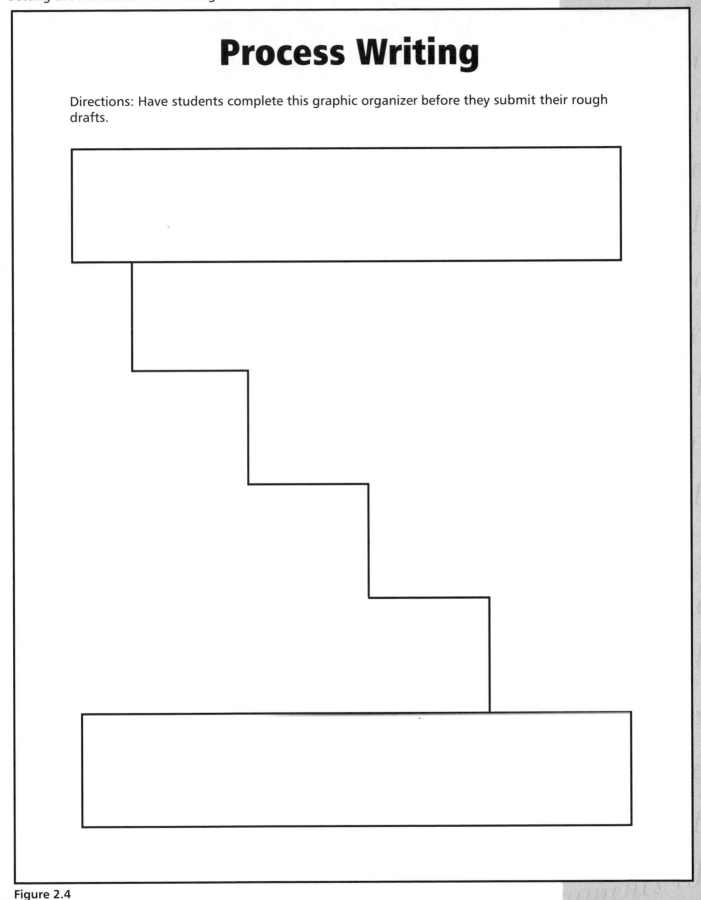

Figure 2.4

Cause/Effect

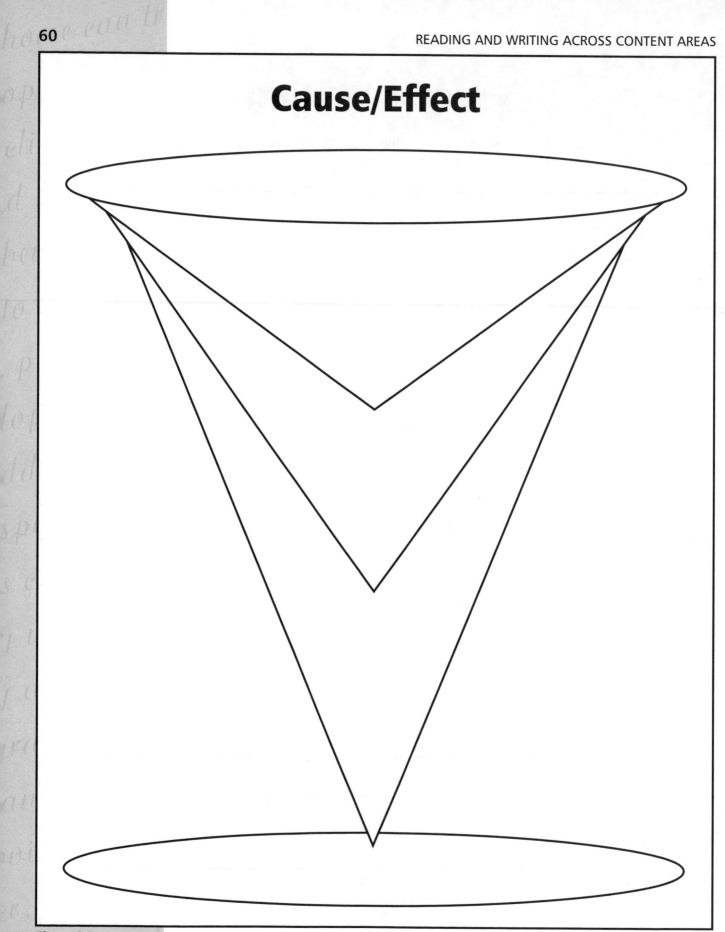

Figure 2.5

Comparison/Contrast

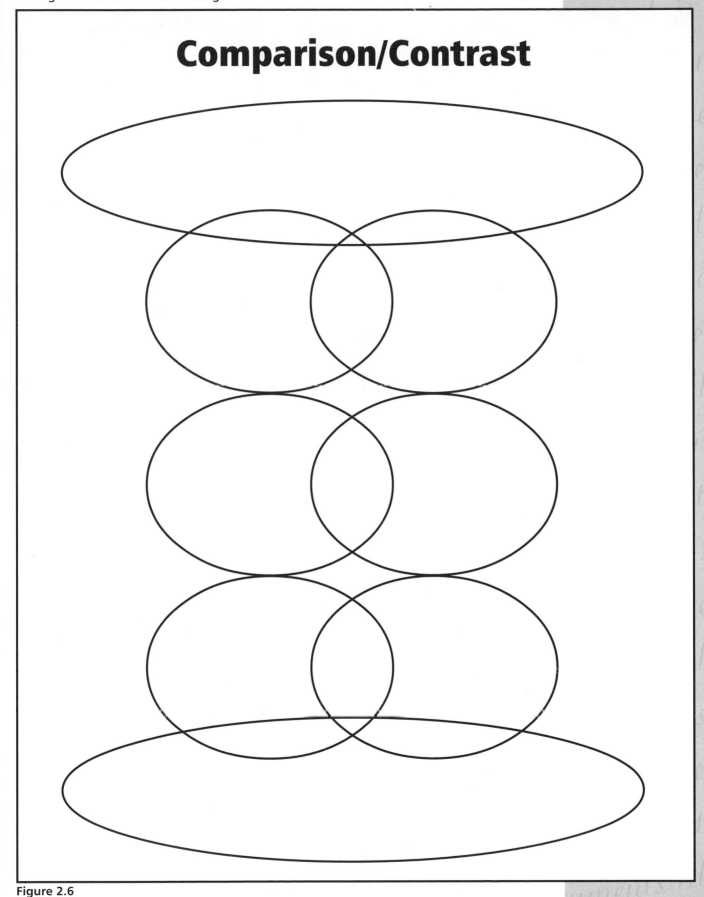

Figure 2.6

CHAPTER 3

Keying into Vocabulary

As our vocabulary expands, so does our power to think . . .

Madeleine L'Engle

PRINCIPLES OF EFFECTIVE VOCABULARY INSTRUCTION

TEACHER-CENTERED STRATEGIES
- Semantic Feature Analysis *
- OPIN
- The Frayer Model*
- Analogies*
- In and Out

STUDENT-CENTERED STRATEGIES
- Clues and Questions
- Kinesthetic Vocabulary
- Concept of Definition*
- Vocabulary Overview Guide*
- Four-Dimensional Study*
- Vocabulary Graphics

CHAPTER SUMMARY

*Indicates that a Blackline Master is included in Teacher Tips at the end of the chapter.

PRINCIPLES OF EFFECTIVE VOCABULARY INSTRUCTION

At some time or another, most classroom teachers have heard students say that they cannot read a story because the words are "too hard." Students brave enough to muddle through the story may skip the difficult words entirely and try unsuccessfully to make sense of the skeletal remains of the story. Stahl (1986) reports that the strongest predictor of a text's difficulty is the number of complex, or challenging, words it contains. He further points out that a review of fifty-two vocabulary instruction studies shows that teaching students the vocabulary words pertinent to the assigned text generally improves their comprehension. Therefore, it makes sense for classroom educators to teach vocabulary. But is one vocabulary strategy as successful as the next? If not, then what characteristics should a successful strategy have?

Vacca and Vacca (1996) contend that students can easily learn the concepts in a unit if teachers link the ideas presented in the chapter to students' prior knowledge. When students can associate a new term with information or a concept they already know, they are more likely to remember the meaning of the word. Stahl (1986) calls this process *association,* and it occurs when a student can link the new term to a synonym or to a familiar context. Another process, *generation,* occurs when students are able to link the association they have made to a new product. These products may include: creating a novel sentence, designing a semantic map, drawing a picture, or creating a set of clue words or phrases to remind them of the word's meaning.

With these characteristics in mind, teachers can design a variety of strategies to help students learn vocabulary terms and connect those terms to their own knowledge and experiences. In our interactions with students, we have found that the following guidelines maximize the effects of teaching vocabulary:

1. Limit the choice of words to those that are essential to the understanding of the reading selection.
2. Categorize the words to be taught and teach them in clusters.
3. Introduce the words prior to having students read the selection.
4. Clarify and refine the definitions by consulting a dictionary.
5. Give students multiple opportunities to practice using the new vocabulary terms.
6. As a way of enriching vocabulary study, help students find creative ways to use synonyms, antonyms, graphics, pantomime, and mapping to learn words.

By and large, there are two types of vocabulary strategies; those that are teacher-centered, which are largely initiated through teacher-led discussion and modeling, and those that are student-directed, which are largely initiated by student thinking. Following are examples of both of these types.

TEACHER-CENTERED STRATEGIES

While it is the goal of every teacher that students become self-directed learners, we also know that direct instruction has a valuable place in our teaching repertoire. Teaching content area vocabulary often involves teaching students concepts rather than merely definitions, and this is usually best accomplished through teacher-centered instruction and modeling. If teachers introduce relevant concepts before teaching a unit, they set a framework for the content and can utilize strategies to help students learn the major concepts.

How do you like this for a vocabulary sentence? My eccentric aunt lives in a musty, rancid, dilapidated, decrepit dwelling!

Semantic Feature Analysis

A major concern in teaching content area vocabulary is how to help students understand concepts and discriminate between related words in a given discipline. Semantic Feature Analysis (Johnson and Pearson 1984) accomplishes this by helping students to focus on the key characteristics of the concept words and identify how those characteristics are shared between words. The use of a graphic organizer helps students see the relationships easily and provides a springboard for discussion on the shared properties of the words. Semantic Feature Analysis is an excellent vehicle to activate students' prior knowledge about content area terms. It helps students learn their definitions, can also be an effective review or assessment technique, and fosters the verbal/linguistic, visual/spatial, logical/mathematical, interpersonal, and intrapersonal intelligences.

Steps in a Semantic Feature Analysis

See Teacher Tips at the end of this chapter for a Blackline Master to use with this strategy (Figure 3.9).

1. Select a content area category or topic that has two or more similar items.
2. Create a matrix by listing the category terms along the left side.
3. List common characteristics, features, or topics across the top.
4. Distribute the matrix to the students and ask them to mark a plus (+) in the blank when the characteristic is present and a minus (-) when it is not.
5. When the matrix is complete, ask students to make generalizations and draw some conclusions about the concepts they have studied.
6. When students have become comfortable in their use of this strategy, invite them to brainstorm common characteristics as you develop the matrix together.

For examples of how to use this strategy in a foreign language classroom, see Figure 3.1a for an activity about items of clothing and the seasons; for ways to use it in physical education classes, see Figure 3.1b.

Semantic Feature Analysis for Spanish				
Categories	**Common Characteristics, Features, or Topics**			
	primavera	otoño	verano	invierno
pantalones	−	+	−	+
pantalones cortos	+	−	+	−
camisa	+	+	+	+
abrigo	−	+	−	+
botas	−	+	−	+
zapatos	+	+	+	+
chaqueta	−	+	−	−
traje de baño	−	−	+	−

Developed by Athena Petras, Prospect Heights District 23, MacArthur Middle School, Prospect Heights, Illinois.

Figure 3.1a

Semantic Feature Analysis for Physical Education					
Categories	Common Characteristics, Features, or Topics				
	Muscular Endurance	Agility	Cardiovascular	Flexibility	Muscular Strength
Sit-ups	+	−	−	−	−
Mile run	+	−	+	−	−
Sit-n-reach	−	−	−	+	−
Pull-ups	−	−	−	−	+
Shuttle run	−	+	−	−	−
Flex arm hang	−	−	−	−	+
Football	−	−	−	−	+
Shot put	−	−	−	−	+
Hurdles	−	−	−	+	+
Hockey	+	+	−	+	−
Soccer	+	+	+	−	−
Swimming	+	−	+	+	−
Volleyball	−	+	−	−	+
Archery	−	−	−	−	+
Wall climbing	+	−	−	+	−
Cycling	+	−	+	−	−
In-line skating	+	−	+	−	−
Developed by Michele Burnett, St. Xavier University's Field-Based Master's Program, Prospect Heights, Illinois.					

Figure 3.1b

OPIN

OPIN (developed by Frank Greene as found in Vacca and Vacca 1996) is a teacher-directed strategy that provides reinforcement for content area vocabulary learning. As its name suggests, it is based on the concept of giving an opinion; the strategy is initiated by the teacher who identifies key terms from the reading and creates sentences to convey their meaning, leaving out the actual term. Students work individually to give their opinions of words that might fit the context of the sentence. The teacher then assigns students to groups of three and tells them to convince the other group members that their opinion is best. Of course, students must provide valid arguments for their choices. If the group is unable to come to a consensus about the meaning of a term, individual members of the group present justification for their selections. When all groups have reached consensus, they share their findings with the whole class. The OPIN strategy works well in any content area and also fosters the verbal/linguistic, logical/mathematical, interpersonal, and intrapersonal intelligences.

The following examples show how to use this strategy with mathematics, science, and social studies.

EXAMPLES OF OPIN FOR MATHEMATICS

1. A linear _____ can be used to show the distance traveled by a runner from the start to finish line. (mile)
2. Since measurements are often written in very small or very large numbers, scientists often rely on scientific _____ to record numerical information. (notation)

EXAMPLES OF OPIN FOR SCIENCE

1. Geese often _____ from northern Canada to the southern United States. (migrate)
2. As the boy scanned the sky, he saw the Earth cross in front of the moon during a _____ eclipse. (lunar)

EXAMPLES OF OPIN FOR SOCIAL STUDIES

1. An _____ is often said to form a type of land bridge between two continents. (isthmus)
2. To learn how people get along together, researchers often study _____. (society)

The Frayer Model

The Frayer Model (Frayer, Frederick, and Klausmeier 1969) is a strategy designed to help students understand content area concepts by identifying both essential and nonessential characteristics of the concept and providing examples for both. A graphic organizer, which can easily by reproduced on any size index card, allows students to visually represent these characteristics and examples, thus fostering the visual/spatial and logical/mathematical intelligences.

 Steps in the Frayer Model

See Teacher Tips at the end of this chapter for a Blackline Master to use with this strategy (Figure 3.10).

1. Introduce an important concept to be learned.
2. Have students brainstorm to generate examples of the concept.
3. Next, instruct students to consult the text and read to locate and/or predict:
   a. additional examples of the concept
   b. essential characteristics
   c. nonessential characteristics
4. Record this newly discovered information on the graphic organizer.
5. Encourage students to share their graphic organizers after their reading. Tell them to confirm or reject the information recorded in a group setting.
6. Develop a master list of the concept, the essential and nonessential characteristics, and appropriate examples; hang a copy in the classroom to reinforce what has been learned.

See Figure 3.2a for an example of how to use the Frayer Model with mathematics; see Figure 3.2b for an example of how to use it with social studies.

Frayer Model for Mathematics

Essential Characteristics	Nonessential Characteristics
• a squared term • no higher power than 2 • y = (quadratic function) • $a\# $ = (quadratic function)	• a linear term • a constant term • numerical coefficients • leading coefficients positive or negative

Concept Word
quadratic

Examples	Nonexamples
• $y = 2x - 4x + 3$ • $x - 5x - 6 = 0$ • $y = x$ • $y = a(x - h) + k$	• $y = mx + b$ • $x - 2x = 3x - 6 = 5$ • $x = 17$

Developed by Laura Butler, Willowbrook High School, Villa Park, Illinois.

Figure 3.2a

Frayer Model for Social Studies

Essential Characteristics	Nonessential Characteristics
• responsibility • independence • makes decisions • stands by choices • economically independent • doesn't blame others	• gender • income • insight • popularity • physical characteristics • age

Concept Word
autonomy

Examples	Nonexamples
• teacher • responsible student • parents	• baby • adult whose mother does his or her laundry • a pet

Figure 3.2b

Analogies

How many times have you heard these comparisons: "The stars are like diamonds" or "She is as quiet as a mouse"? These two similes are easy to understand and to visualize. The analogy, like the simile and metaphor, is based on points of comparison. It is a form of logical inference, based on the assumption that two concepts relate in some respects. Students need to be able to understand the relationships of the concepts and restate them in their own words; thus, analogies promote critical thinking skills and relate to the verbal/linguistic, intrapersonal, and logical/mathematical intelligences. Buehl and Hein (1990) created an analogy graphic organizer to help students visualize the similarities and differences between a concept and something that is familiar to their lives. This strategy, like the others described in this text, works best if teachers provide an example and guide their students through the steps.

 Steps for Creating Analogies

See Teacher Tips at the end of this chapter for a Blackline Master to use with this strategy (Figure 3.11).

1. Select a concept from the content area and explain how it relates to a concept that the students recognize. For example, in a social studies class, you could compare the role of the US Congress to the role of a school principal.

2. Place the graphic organizer on an overhead projector. Ask individuals or small groups to identify examples that are common to both concepts. Record answers in that portion of the graphic organizer.

3. Now ask students to think about both concepts and identify differences they have. Record those answers in that portion of the graphic organizer.

4. Next, ask students to identify categories (e.g., "rule making") that comprise the basis for comparison.

See Figure 3.3 for an example of how to use this valuable strategy.

Analogies	
Similarities and Differences Between Concepts of:	
Congress and School Principal	
Similarities	**Differences**
Congress and principals both set rules and regulations.	Congress has more members and rules and regulations.
Both organizations need to work together to achieve goals.	Congress has nationwide goals.
Neither has complete power regarding issues.	Congress has Senate and president; principal has superintendent and school board.
Both organizations represent other groups of people.	Congress rules the nation; principal rules the school community.
Both have committees.	Congress has joint committees; principals have assistants and parent advisors.
Both have processes for achieving goals.	Congress votes; principal makes rulings based on input from others.

Figure 3.3

In and Out

This vocabulary strategy replicates Marzano's (1992) concept attainment model that asks students to determine the characteristics of a category by using reasoning skills. The basic premise of this strategy is to help students find a pattern in the characteristics of a particular content and to identify the items by pairing like examples against nonexamples. While this strategy is particularly effective in science and social studies classes, it also works with vocabulary instruction. Teachers choose related words from a unit of instruction and present them, one at a time, on an overhead projector or on a blackboard until the students can identify similar terms. Although the focus of this strategy is not on the meaning of the words but on the ability to recognize similar terms, students need to understand the meaning in order to identify similar words in that category. This strategy asks students to use their prior knowledge of terms, associate like terms, and make connections. It fosters the verbal/linguistic, logical/mathematical, interpersonal, intrapersonal, and visual/spatial intelligences.

Steps for the In and Out Vocabulary Strategy

1. Choose five to ten related words from a unit of study.
2. Write the words "In" and "Out" on an overhead projector or on a blackboard.
3. Present the words one at a time, giving the correct example (In) first, and then giving a nonexample (Out). Write the words in the appropriate category.
4. Continue the process until the students identify the related words.

Refer to Figure 3.4 for an example of how to use the In and Out Strategy for art.

In and Out for Art	
IN = Still Life	**OUT = Landscape**
apple	mountains
bottle	field
table	trail
bowl	path
Cezanne	Monet

Figure 3.4

STUDENT-CENTERED STRATEGIES

Recent research on the brain indicates that the hippocampus, the portion of the brain that decides whether to store information in long-term memory or discard it, is more apt to store information if it links that data with prior knowledge or with emotional significance. Thus, vocabulary strategies that utilize either one or both of these elements lend themselves to helping students remember new words more efficiently. The following strategies require that students use an emotional hook, such as illustration or pantomime, as well as their prior knowledge, to develop examples of the words they are learning. Thus, they are student-centered strategies.

Clues and Questions

Clues and Questions (Readence, Bean, and Baldwin 1998) is another technique that is effective both as a teaching and a review strategy. Using concept area words, the teacher and students develop a set of clues and questions about each word; then, the teacher challenges students to define selected words in a game format.

Steps for Clues and Questions Activity

1. Determine the content area vocabulary words to be learned and write them on index cards.

2. Distribute a card to each student and ask them to write questions that can be answered by using the vocabulary words on the cards.

3. Encourage students to use their prior knowledge, textbooks, and any other information they might have to discern the definition of the words and then develop their questions.

4. Assign students to small groups, and tell them to proceed in a round-robin format. Follow these steps for the activity:

   a. A selected student should pick a card without looking at it and show the word to the group.

   b. This student must listen to the other group members who take turns asking questions or giving clues until the word is defined.

5. Continue the process until all the students in the group have had a turn. Conclude the game when all the words have been defined.

See the following for ways to use Clues and Questions in your classroom.

CLUES AND QUESTIONS FOR SCIENCE AND SOCIAL STUDIES

linear

1. This is a type of measurement used to show the distance traveled by a runner from start to finish in a race.

2. It is a unit to measure length.

3. What would you use to measure the distance of a marathon racecourse?

4. What type of measurement is used to measure along a straight line?

notation

1. This is a method of measuring used by scientists.

2. It records numerical information when very small or very large numbers are needed.

3. If you were a scientist, what would you use to record the numbers in your experiment?

migrate

1. This term means "moving from one region in the country to the other."

2. Animals and birds do this to avoid inclement weather.

3. What do Canadian geese and most other birds do to escape the cold weather?

lunar

1. This word pertains to the moon.
2. It can be a type of eclipse.
3. What astrological word can be considered the opposite of solar?

isthmus

1. This body of land is formed between two continents.
2. What do we call a bridge of land that connects continents?
3. There is one of these between two continents.

society

1. This term refers to groups of people who live together.
2. It is a group of people who have some common characteristics.
3. Without this, the peoples of the world would be less civilized.

Kinesthetic Vocabulary

Kinesthetic Vocabulary (Lazear 1999), like the other vocabulary acquisition strategies discussed in this chapter, requires students to relate to the target word on a personal level while also fostering the verbal/linguistic, bodily/kinesthetic, interpersonal, and intrapersonal intelligences. To use this vocabulary strategy, students work in cooperative groups of three, using the following procedure.

 Steps for Kinesthetic Vocabulary

1. Distribute words to student teams.
2. Tell students that each member should learn the assigned words and then decide on the best action or pantomime to teach the word to the group.
3. Once students become confident about the vocabulary terms, tell them to teach their words to the rest of the group. Have them follow these directions:
    a. Show the word to the group and have them repeat it.
    b. Act out the word to the group and have them repeat the action.
    c. Check for understanding.
4. When all students feel confident about the words learned, call out each word. Instruct students to do the learned action while repeating the word and meaning.

Following are some helpful terms to use in Kinesthetic Vocabulary.

WORDS TO USE IN KINESTHETIC VOCABULARY

Science	Social Studies	Mathematics	Art/Music
stimulus	colony	concentric circles	bass cleft
solar	treaty	unequal	symphony
nucleus	banned	equation	texture
respiration	autocratic	parallel	pastel
theory	monarch	trapezoid	free-form

Concept of Definition

Sometimes words are elusive. We think we know what a word means only to discover we are not quite on target and that a simple definition is often not enough. Consider the administrator who introduces a faculty member as one of the oldest on staff! We all know he would have exhibited far more tact had he referred to the venerable staff member as one of the most experienced. The only way to be sure we understand the full meaning of a word is to understand not only its denotations but its connotations as well—its subtle meanings and the specific contexts in which it can occur. A vocabulary strategy that fosters this kind of deep understanding of words is the Concept of Definition (Schwartz and Raphael 1985). This strategy utilizes a graphic organizer to encourage students to delve into the word. Students become aware of the types of information that contribute to the meaning of a word. They integrate this data into their own prior knowledge by generating a description and examples of the concept word.

 Steps for Concept of Definition

See Teacher Tips at the end of this chapter for a Blackline Master to use with this strategy (Figure 3.12).

1. Present a new term or concept that students are to learn.

2. Place the word in the center of the Concept of Definition map.

3. Next, instruct students to consult their texts, a glossary, or a dictionary (individually or in small groups) to complete the remaining parts of the concept map using the following guidelines:

   a. Determine to what category the word belongs and place it in the section of the concept map labeled "What Is It?"

b. Identify the word's characteristics or properties and place these in the sections of the concept map labeled "What Is It Like?"

4. Have students brainstorm examples of the word from their own background knowledge. Tell them to place this information in the section of the concept map labeled "What Are Some Examples?"

Figure 3.5a shows how this strategy can be used with math; Figure 3.5b shows how it can be used with science.

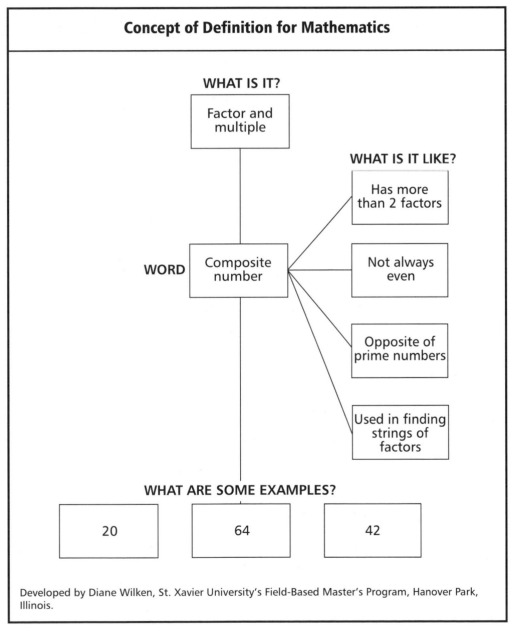

Concept of Definition for Mathematics

WHAT IS IT?
Factor and multiple

WHAT IS IT LIKE?
Has more than 2 factors

WORD — Composite number

Not always even

Opposite of prime numbers

Used in finding strings of factors

WHAT ARE SOME EXAMPLES?
20   64   42

Developed by Diane Wilken, St. Xavier University's Field-Based Master's Program, Hanover Park, Illinois.

Figure 3.5a

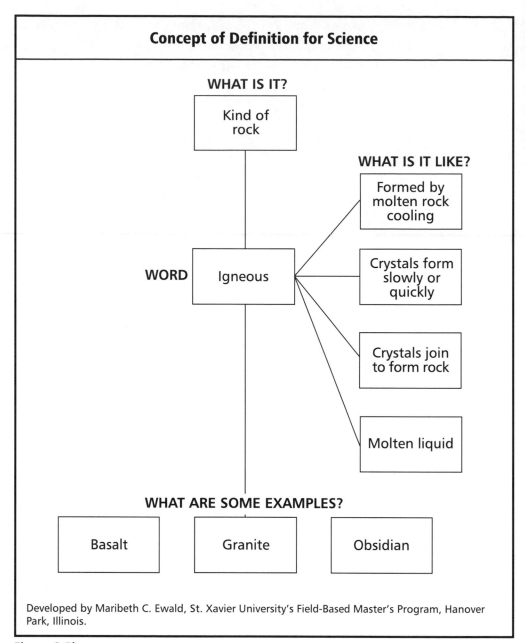

Concept of Definition for Science

WHAT IS IT?

Kind of rock

WHAT IS IT LIKE?

WORD — Igneous

Formed by molten rock cooling

Crystals form slowly or quickly

Crystals join to form rock

Molten liquid

WHAT ARE SOME EXAMPLES?

Basalt   Granite   Obsidian

Developed by Maribeth C. Ewald, St. Xavier University's Field-Based Master's Program, Hanover Park, Illinois.

Figure 3.5b

Vocabulary Overview Guide

The Vocabulary Overview Guide (Carr 1985) is a vocabulary strategy that places the responsibility of learning new words from content areas on the students. It encourages them to connect these new terms to their prior knowledge by including an important clue to the word's meaning as part of the graphic organizer that accompanies the strategy. Since the students must complete the Overview Guide as they read their text, it conditions them to be alert to key words in the reading and also provides a structured system for studying those words (Buehl 1995). As always, for best results, the teacher should model this strategy before students use it independently.

 ### Steps for Vocabulary Overview Guide

See Teacher Tips at the end of this chapter for a Blackline Master to use with this strategy (Figure 3.13).

1. With the students, clarify the main topic or theme of the selection or text to be read.

2. After previewing the selection, have students determine what categories of words might be found in the selection that relate to the topic/theme. These categories are written on the Overview Guide.

3. Instruct students to read the text and identify words that have some connection to the topic/theme. These are written as keywords under the appropriate category on the Overview Guide and then defined using the text, a glossary, or a dictionary.

4. As a last step, have students brainstorm possible clues to help them learn each new word. In order to assure a link between the new word and their existing prior knowledge, encourage students to select clues that have some personal meaning to them.

Figure 3.6a offers a Vocabulary Overview Guide for science; Figure 3.6b offers a Vocabulary Overview Guide for social studies.

Vocabulary Overview Guide for Science		
TOPIC Energy **CATEGORY** Renewable Energy		
Word: solar energy	**Word:** fossil fuel	**Word:** hydropower
Definition: Using the energy of the sun.	**Definition:** A burnable material formed over millions of years.	**Definition:** Using the energy of falling water.
Clue: My solar calculator won't work in the dark.	**Clue:** coal	**Clue:** Niagara Falls

Figure 3.6a

Vocabulary Overview Guide for Social Studies		
TOPIC _____ Society _____ **CATEGORY** _____ Caste System _____		
Word: untouchable	**Word:** Brahmans	**Word:** caste
Definition: The lowest level of Indian society; to touch members of this group defiles you.	**Definition:** Priests, scholars, and wise men in the Indian society.	**Definition:** Smaller, leveled groups within a society's structure.
Clue: Like acid (or maybe a freshman?)	**Clue:** Pastor John	**Clue:** Classes in a high school

Figure 3.6b

Four-Dimensional Study

Standard practice asks students to learn the meaning of vocabulary terms by memorizing the dictionary definition. While all learning depends on memory, students cannot always remember memorized vocabulary terms because they do not link the terms to their prior knowledge or to other terms they know. The Four-Dimensional Study strategy encourages students to learn each vocabulary term by using four different approaches: context clues, dictionary definitions, creating an application, and visual. It also promotes the use of the verbal/linguistic, intrapersonal, interpersonal, and visual/spatial intelligences.

 Steps for Four-Dimensional Study

See Teacher Tips at the end of this chapter for a Blackline Master to use with this strategy (Figure 3.14).

1. Choose five to ten words from the text that are unfamiliar to the students.

2. Instruct students to follow this procedure on an index card:
   a. On the top of the card, copy the sentence that contains the vocabulary word. Underline the target word.
   b. Determine the meaning of the word through context clues or dictionary or glossary use, and write it on the left-hand side of the card.

   c. Write a personal knowledge or experience example of the word on the right-hand side of the card.
   d. Draw a picture or a symbol related to the word.

Refer to Figure 3.7 for an example of Four-Dimensional Study.

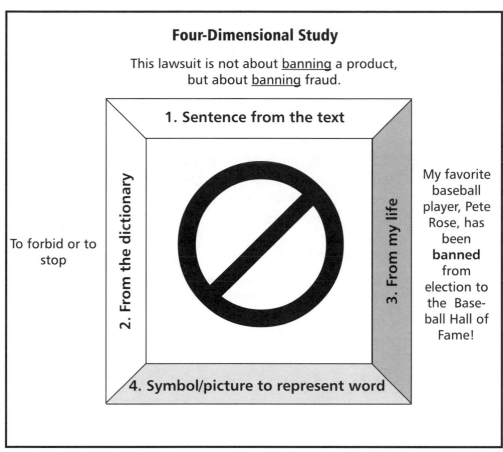

Four-Dimensional Study

This lawsuit is not about <u>banning</u> a product, but about <u>banning</u> fraud.

1. Sentence from the text

2. From the dictionary

To forbid or to stop

3. From my life

My favorite baseball player, Pete Rose, has been **banned** from election to the Base-ball Hall of Fame!

4. Symbol/picture to represent word

Figure 3.7

Vocabulary Graphics

This strategy and its variations ask students to create an illustration for the word they are learning which appeals to the visual/spatial intelligence.

 Steps for Vocabulary Graphics

1. Give students 5×7 index cards upon which to record their findings.
2. Instruct students to use their background knowledge, information from the text, glossary, or a dictionary to determine the definition.

Have students write the word and its definition in the center of the card.

3. Tell students to record the following information in each of the card's four corners:
   a. a sentence using the word
   b. a synonym for the word
   c. an antonym for the word
   d. an illustration that represents the word. Encourage students to create an illustration that has some personal significance to them.

4. You can hook the index cards together with a binder ring so that they become a permanent student vocabulary file.

For a variation on the Vocabulary Graphics strategy, advise students to record the information on a plastic transparency or a sheet of newsprint. When complete, ask students to present their graphics to the class, explaining their relation to the word and its significance to them. An added benefit of this strategy is that it also fosters the verbal/linguistic, bodily/kinesthetic, interpersonal, and intrapersonal intelligences. See Figure 3.8 for an example of Vocabulary Graphics.

Example of Vocabulary Graphics

SENTENCE:
When I think of a NUCLEUS, I think of a sunny-side up egg!

SYNONYM:
core

WORD: Nucleus
DEFINITION: A nucleus is the center

ILLUSTRATION:

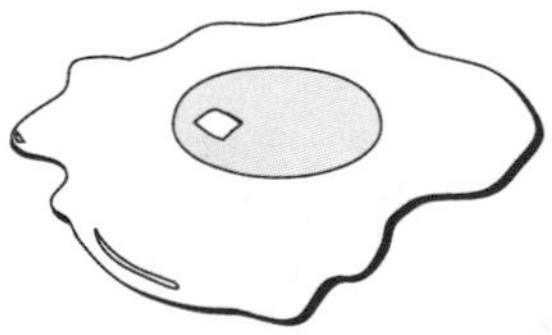

ANTONYM:
edge

Figure 3.8

CHAPTER SUMMARY

In order for students to successfully comprehend content area subjects, they need to understand the vocabulary in their texts. Chapter 3 described both teacher-centered and student-centered vocabulary strategies. Teacher-centered strategies include: Semantic Feature Analysis, OPIN, The Frayer Model, Analogies, and In and Out. Student-centered strategies include: Clues and Questions, Kinesthetic Vocabulary, Concept of Definition, Vocabulary Overview Guide, Four-Dimensional Study, and Vocabulary Graphics.

COMPUTER CONNECTIONS

1. Assign students into teams or groups. Using either the strategies OPIN or Clues and Questions, have them create the examples using the computer. When all the OPIN or Clues and Questions examples are completed, have the teams or groups compete to answer each other's questions. The team or group that accrues the greatest number of points wins.

2. Assign individual students three to five vocabulary words from the chapter. Then, using either the Vocabulary Graphics or Four-Dimensional Study strategies, have students create a template that fulfills the parameters of the strategy and illustrates the word using computer graphics or clip art. These can be saved by the teacher and printed out for student review and practice.

Teacher Tips

❶ As students use the various strategies to develop their vocabulary examples, be sure to either make copies or collect the original work to use as examples when you explain the procedures to future students.

❷ Use the Blackline Masters provided for the following strategies:

    a.   Semantic Feature Analysis (Figure 3.9)

    b.   Frayer Model (Figure 3.10)

    c.   Analogies (Figure 3.11)

    d.   Concept of Definition (Figure 3.12)

    e.   Vocabulary Overview Guide (Figure 3.13)

    f.   Four Dimensional Study (Figure 3.14)

Semantic Feature Analysis

Directions: Your teacher will provide a list of concepts you are studying. Mark a plus (+) in the blank when the characteristic is present in this particular concept and a minus (-) when it is not. Using this matrix, try to make generalizations and draw some conclusions about the concepts you have studied.

Categories	Common Characteristics, Features, or Topics			

Based on Johnson and Pearson 1984.

Figure 3.9

The Frayer Model

Write the name of the concept you are studying in the space provided. Consult your text and read to locate and/or predict additional essential characteristics, nonessential characteristics, examples, and non-examples of the concept. Record this newly discovered information on the graphic organizer.

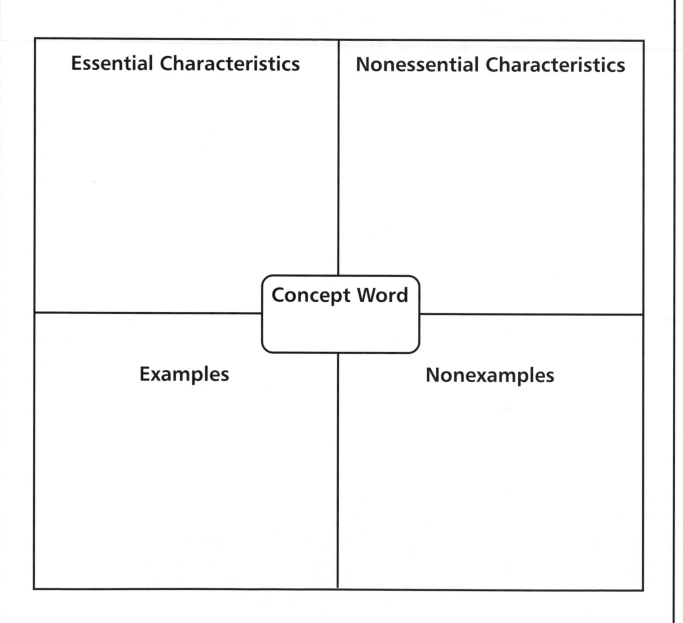

Essential Characteristics

Nonessential Characteristics

Concept Word

Examples

Nonexamples

Based on Frayer, Frederick, and Klausmeir 1969.

Figure 3.10

Analogies

Directions: Select two concepts from the content area you are studying. Identify examples that are common to both concepts and record them under similarities in the graphic organizer below. Then identify examples that are different and record them under differences.

SIMILARITIES AND DIFFERENCES BETWEEN CONCEPTS OF:

SIMILARITIES	DIFFERENCES

Figure 3.11

Concept of Definition

Directions: Write the new term or concept that you are learning in the center of the Concept of Definition map. Consult your texts, a glossary, or a dictionary (individually or in small groups) to complete the remaining parts of the concept map. Be sure to provide some good examples.

Concept of Definition for _____

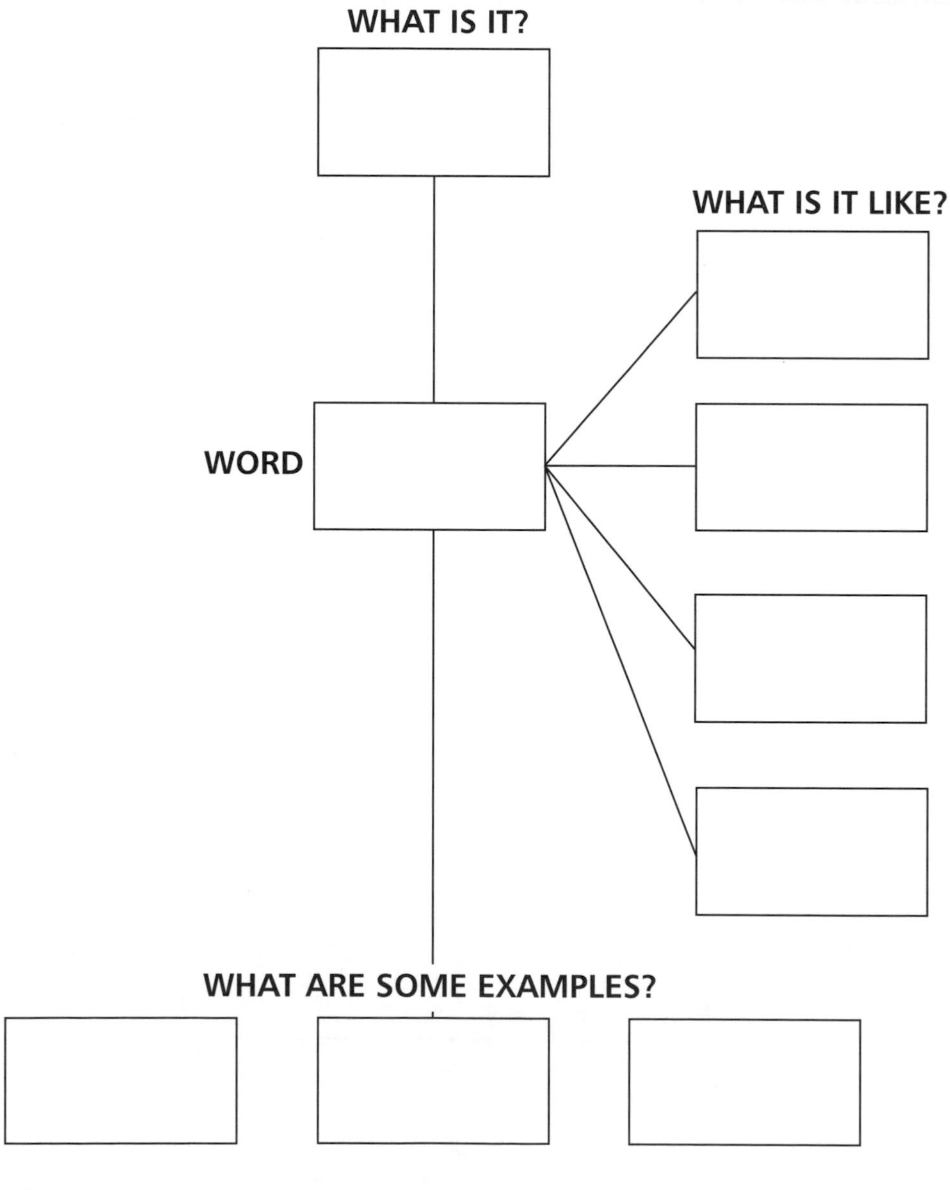

WHAT IS IT?

WHAT IS IT LIKE?

WORD

WHAT ARE SOME EXAMPLES?

Based on Schwartz and Raphael 1985.

Figure 3.12

Vocabulary Overview Guide

Directions: Determine the main topic of the selection to be read and to which category it belongs. Read the text and identify words that have some connection to the topic/theme. Write these as keywords under the appropriate category on the Vocabulary Overview Guide and then define them using the text, a glossary, or a dictionary. Brainstorm possible clues to help you learn each new word. Be sure to select clues that have some personal meaning for you.

Vocabulary Overview Guide for _____

TOPIC _____ CATEGORY _____		
Word:	Word:	Word:
Definition:	Definition:	Definition:
Clue:	Clue:	Clue:

Based on Carr 1985.

Figure 3.13

Four-Dimensional Study

Directions: Copy a sentence from the text that contains the vocabulary word. Underline the target word. Determine the meaning of the word through context clues or dictionary or glossary use, and write it on the space provided. Then, write a personal knowledge or experience example of the word. Draw a picture or a symbol related to the word in the box.

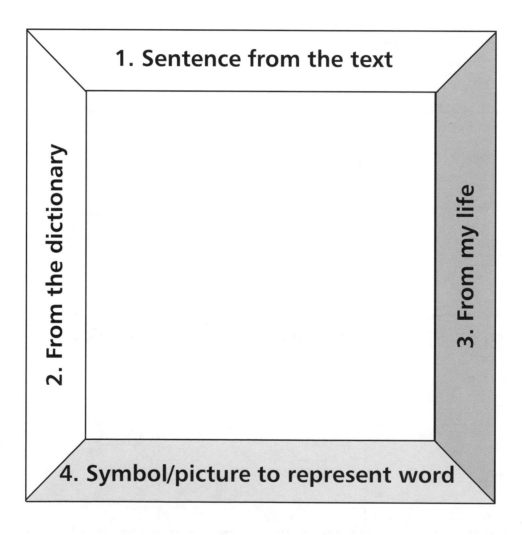

1. Sentence from the text

2. From the dictionary

3. From my life

4. Symbol/picture to represent word

Figure 3.14

Strategies for Comprehension

Reading is to the mind what exercise is to the body.

Sir Richard Steele

WHAT MAKES A STRATEGIC READER?

THE READING PROCESS

PREREADING STRATEGIES
- Word Association
- Brain Writing
- Knowledge Rating*
- Anticipation/Prediction Guides
- Directed Reading-Thinking Activity (DRTA)
- Sketch to Stretch*

DURING READING STRATEGIES
- Note Taking
  - Main Idea I*
  - Structured Note Taking
- Study/Reading Guides
  - Three Level Guide
  - Point of View Study Guide

AFTER READING STRATEGIES
- Cubing
- Perspective Cubing
- Magnet Summaries*
- Socratic Questioning

CHAPTER SUMMARY

*Indicates that a Blackline Master is included in Teacher Tips at the end of the chapter.

WHAT MAKES A STRATEGIC READER?

When Roberta Sejnost was a young child, her mother thought she was a strategic reader because she was a fluent oral reader. Teachers thought she was a strategic reader because she completed all her comprehension worksheets correctly. Her younger sister was convinced Roberta was a strategic reader because Roberta could read bigger books than she could read. However, no one seemed to have a specific definition of what a strategic reader really was or an idea of how a student could become one. In truth, parents, classroom teachers, and researchers have sought to characterize the strategic reader for decades. Paris, Lipson, and Wixson (1983) note that strategic readers are people who are in control of their reading because they move through a series of steps in the reading process: analysis, planning, monitoring, and regulating.

First, strategic readers analyze the task before them by understanding the reading demands made of them and setting a purpose for their reading. In other words, they are able to identify the type of text (narrative or expository) as well as the reading goal to be accomplished. They can read the first chapter or the entire selection. They can readily identify their purpose as reading for pleasure or reading to answer test questions. Next, they are able to initiate a plan of action to achieve that purpose by choosing the strategies they will use as they read. For example, they might choose to skim the material first, identifying the text patterns used; then reread it, making predictions as they go; and finally end by summarizing what they have read. As strategic readers move through this process, they monitor and regulate their comprehension. They recognize that comprehension is occurring because they understand what they are reading. By the same token, if they suddenly become aware that they no longer understand, they know what to do to repair or fix their comprehension problem by rereading a passage, looking up an unfamiliar vocabulary word, or asking a teacher for help. Similarly, if comprehension is progressing well, they may skip sections that contain irrelevant or extraneous details or skim over a passage that contains familiar material.

THE READING PROCESS

As classroom teachers, we are all anxious to help our students develop as strategic readers. Thus, we need to consider what we can do to best foster the strategic reader characteristics described above.

When Roberta first began teaching, she tried to make her students into strategic readers by using the traditional format of lesson presentation that she had learned in her methods courses; namely, she assigned a reading and held students accountable for reading it. Then she culminated the lesson by holding a discussion to see if students learned what she had wanted them to learn. Ultimately, they did not always learn what she had wanted them to learn; worse yet, there were times when they had not even read the assignment.

The good news is that today we know the traditional format is outmoded. No longer is class discussion the primary gauge of reading comprehension. Current educational research supports a format that identifies three stages of reading first observed by Robinson in 1978: *before the text is read, while the text is being read,* and *after the eyes have left the page.* Prereading activities are offered as the first level of support. These activities involve fostering students' prior knowledge. *Prereading* makes students aware of the text structure, helps them identify a purpose for reading, clarifies the vocabulary demands that the text will make, and preteaches a concept that may be difficult. Most importantly, it piques student interest in the reading material.

In the second stage, *during reading,* students interact with their text. In order to make this interaction effective, teachers encourage students to make predictions, keep their purpose for reading in mind, and self-monitor their understanding. Teachers should encourage students to make connections between what they are reading (new knowledge) and what they already know (old knowledge). Instructional frameworks (study guides, graphic organizers) created or provided by the teacher help students accomplish these tasks efficiently. These instructional frameworks are a viable strategy to use in this stage of the reading process.

Finally, in the last stage of the process, *after reading,* students clarify, reinforce, and extend what they have learned. During this stage, students need to organize, synthesize, analyze, and evaluate what they have read so they can easily understand and retrieve important information. In effect, this stage of the reading process allows students to show what they have learned through discussions, presentations, writing activities, research activities, and performances.

PREREADING STRATEGIES

As noted earlier, students use prereading strategies before they actually begin reading. The main purpose of these activities is to provide teachers with an opportunity to learn what their students already know about a subject and then help foster adequate prior knowledge so students are mentally ready for instruction. Invaluable as a motivational tool, these activities encourage students to read their assignments.

Word Association

Word Association (Zalaluk, Samuels, and Taylor 1986) is a simple strategy to measure students' prior knowledge about a topic. It is similar to the concept of brainstorming but follows a more definitive procedure. This strategy was developed on the theory that if students have a great deal of prior knowledge about a concept, they should be able to make a number of associations about it. Using this strategy, the teacher supplies students with a keyword and then asks them to make as many associations as they can based on their knowledge of and familiarity with that keyword. Associations can be things, places, events, ideas, etc. However, teachers should discourage students from making associations that are subordinate ideas of the keyword. Focusing on subordinate ideas suggests students are making associations with the words they are generating as associations rather than with the keywords themselves. After students generate the list, the teacher evaluates students' prior knowledge according to the following scale:

0–2 points = low prior knowledge

3–6 points = average prior knowledge

7+ points = high prior knowledge

 Steps for Generating Word Associations

1. Select a keyword from a topic and tell students to write it on the margin of a piece of paper.
2. Give students three minutes to write down as many words as they can that are related to the keyword. Tell them that they may write down things, places, events, ideas, etc.
3. Award student responses one point for every reasonable association.
4. Tally one additional point for a subordinate idea, but allow a student only one additional point no matter how many subordinate ideas they list. Follow this suggestion to discourage students from using generated words rather than keywords.

See Figure 4.1 for an example of this valuable Word Association strategy.

```
┌─────────────────────────────────────────────────────────────────┐
│                   Example of Word Association                     │
├─────────────────────────────────────────────────────────────────┤
│                                                                   │
│   Keyword        Generated Words                                  │
│                                                                   │
│   Shark          Ocean                 Fins                       │
│                  Killer                Nurse Shark                 │
│                  Great White           Tiger Shark                │
│                  Live babies                                      │
│                                                                   │
│   Total points: 5 points                                          │
│        1 point for each generated word: ocean, killer, live       │
│        babies, fins                                               │
│        1 point for all subordinate words: Great White, Nurse      │
│        Shark, Tiger Shark                                         │
│                                                                   │
└─────────────────────────────────────────────────────────────────┘
```

Figure 4.1

Brain Writing

Brain Writing (Rodrigues 1983) is a variation of good old-fashioned brainstorming; however, it follows a more organized procedure and is thus effective in fostering prior knowledge as well as assessing what students already know about a topic.

 Steps for Brain Writing

1. Have students choose a topic (word or concept) about which they will study (research).

2. Instruct students to brainstorm, either individually, in small groups, or as a class, what they know or think they know about the topic and write the information in colored ink on a large sheet of newsprint. (Group breakdown depends on the purpose and structure of the assignment.)

3. Encourage students to share the written information (individuals meet with small group; small group meets with another small group, etc.). After discussion of the information, have students record any additions, corrections, or comments in a different color ink and award points for information added or corrected.

4. (Optional) Invite the whole class to share knowledge and discuss what is known and what needs to be learned.

5. Instruct students to read (research) to verify or refute knowledge. Allow students to work individually or in collaborative groups.

Knowledge Rating

Knowledge Rating (Blachowicz 1991), while often used as a vocabulary strategy, is also an excellent way to foster prior knowledge about a topic to be studied. There are many variations of this strategy; however, the standard procedure for using Knowledge Rating requires the teacher to provide students with a grid that lists the vocabulary words pertinent to the topic being studied. The teacher then instructs students to show their knowledge of the words by marking: "can define," "have heard," "have seen," "can spell," "can say," and so forth, on the grid. Teachers then ask students to analyze each word. However, teachers can also use this procedure effectively to foster students' prior knowledge by taking it a step further following this procedure.

 ### Steps for Using a Knowledge Rating

See Teacher Tips at the end of this chapter for a Blackline Master to use with this strategy (Figure 4.10).

1. Distribute a list of words appropriate to the topic to be studied.

2. Ask students to respond individually to each category by placing an × in the appropriate boxes. Students should be ready to explain or illustrate their responses. Possible categories in addition to those noted above might include "can give an example or an illustration," "can explain," or "can tell how I knew or learned the term."

3. After asking students to respond individually, encourage them to share their responses, first in small groups and then in a whole class discussion.

4. By encouraging students to freely share their responses during the whole class follow-up discussion, the teacher is able to ascertain which terms students know well and foster students' prior knowledge of those terms with which they are unfamiliar.

See Figure 4.2a for an example of how to help your students evaluate their knowledge of science vocabulary; see Figure 4.2b to see how they can evaluate their knowledge of social studies vocabulary terms.

Knowledge Rating for Science

Word	Have Seen or Heard	Can Say	Can Define	Can Spell	Can Use in a Sentence	Don't Know at All
diffusion	X					
permeable						X
glucose	X	X		X		
dialysis	X	X	X	X	X	
endocytosis						X
phagocytosis						X
impermeable						X
osmosis	X	X	X	X	X	

Figure 4.2a

Knowledge Rating for Social Studies

Word	Have Seen or Heard	Can Say	Can Define	Can Spell	Can Use in a Sentence	Don't Know at All
ogliarchy						X
anarchy	X	X	X	X	X	
democracy	X		X			
communism		X		X		
socialism						X
impeachment	X	X				
monarchy		X		X		
banishment	X					

Figure 4.2b

Anticipation/Prediction Guides

Anticipation Guides (Readance, Bean, and Baldwin 1998) or Prediction Guides (Nichols 1983) help students prepare for the reading they will do. These guides ask them to anticipate or make predictions about the content they will read by responding to a series of statements about that content. However, as in the Knowledge Rating strategy discussed earlier, there are many variations of Anticipation/Prediction Guides. Some guides ask students to respond individually, while others ask students to respond as a small group. Furthermore, some Anticipation Guides ask students to respond to illustrations or graphics as well as written statements.

Anticipation/Prediction Guides are valuable for several reasons. First, the strategy provides a springboard for students to consider the topic to be read, thus fostering prior knowledge. Second, it helps focus interest in the topic, motivating students to read the assigned text. Students are much more interested in reading a selection to see if their predictions are correct than in reading it because the teacher told them to! In addition, making predictions and then reading to confirm or reject them helps students set a purpose for reading. Finally, Readence, Bean, and Baldwin (1998) make the following points: since students make their responses prior to reading, they operate from their experiences and belief systems alone, thus allowing them to respond with little fear of failure due to lack of knowledge. In addition, due to their experiences and belief systems, they might hold preconceived misconceptions about some topics that negatively affect learning. Progressing through the prereading, reading, and postreading stages of this strategy helps alert teachers to these misconceptions and allows them to modify students' knowledge accordingly.

 ### Steps for Using Anticipation/Prediction Guides

1. Identify those major concepts or details in the selection that students should know or that may challenge or support students' beliefs. Choose statements that stimulate student thinking and interest by presenting concepts about which they may have many opinions but few facts.

2. Leave space next to statements for students to respond (individually, in small groups, or in the whole group).

3. As each statement is discussed, ask students to justify or defend their opinions. Discourage yes/no responses. As an alternative, ask the class to come to a consensus.

4. Instruct students to read the selection.

5. Tell students to revisit the Anticipation/Prediction Guide to determine if they have changed their minds as a result of reading the

selection. Have students locate sections in the text that support their newfound knowledge.

6. You may wish to include a column for prediction of author's beliefs.

7. You have the option of using graphics instead of statements.

Figures 4.3a, 4.3b, and 4.3c show how Anticipation Guides can be used with health, mathematics, and social studies, respectively.

Anticipation Guide for Health

Anticipation Guide: Smoking

Directions

Before reading pages 194–198 in your health book, read each statement and place a "yes" by those statements with which you agree and a "no" by those statements with which you disagree under the section labeled *Anticipation.* In the appropriate space, write your reasons for agreeing or disagreeing.

Anticipation   **Question**

1._____   Smoking can make a person look cool.
                   Reason:

2._____   Short-term effects of smoking on the body are not that bad.
                   Reason:

3._____   It is easier to enjoy your favorite activities if you do not smoke.
                   Reason:

4._____   Smokeless tobacco is bad for you.
                   Reason:

5._____   Quitting tobacco use is very easy to do.
                   Reason:

Developed by Michele Burnett, St. Xavier University's Field-Based Master's Program, Prospect Heights, Illinois.

Figure 4.3a

Anticipation Guide for Mathematics

Anticipation Guide: Percents

Directions

Before reading pages 318 and 319 in your math book, read each statement and place a "yes" by those statements with which you agree and a "no" by those statements with which you disagree under the section labeled *Anticipation*.

Anticipation	Question
1._____	Decimals are not whole numbers.
2._____	You can recognize a decimal number because it always has a decimal point.
3._____	Decimal numbers are based on the number 10.
4._____	You line up the decimal point in numbers when you add them.
5._____	You always get a larger number when you multiply decimals.
6._____	Decimals are not related to fractions.

Developed by Nancy Costea, Clarendon Hills Middle School, Clarendon Hills, Illinois.

Figure 4.3b

Anticipation Guide for Social Studies

Anticipation Guide : The '60s

Directions

Step 1: Before reading the material dealing with the music of the '60s, read each statement below and put a + by the statements you agree with and a – by the statements you disagree with. You will fill in the column headed "Personal."

Step 2: You will join with other students, share your answers, defend your point of view, but come to consensus and fill in the column headed "Group."

Step 3: Please read the material and fill in the column headed "Author" with a + by statements the author would support.

Personal	Group	Author		
_____	_____	_____	1.	The American people did not accept music from other countries.
_____	_____	_____	2.	Many new types of music were developed in the '60s such as soul, swing, and pop.
_____	_____	_____	3.	Woodstock was a peaceful part of the counterculture revolution.
_____	_____	_____	4.	The Beatles' first hit was "I Wanna Hold Your Hand."
_____	_____	_____	5.	The Beatles made records, starred in movies, and did tours, but did not write any of their own music.
_____	_____	_____	6.	Because World War II was over, there was no need for protest music.
_____	_____	_____	7.	Until the late '50s, "soul" music was not allowed on the radio.
_____	_____	_____	8.	This was the "baby boomer" generation.
_____	_____	_____	9.	Hippies and communes were abundant.
_____	_____	_____	10.	About 2,000 attended Woodstock.

Developed by Douglas Sommers, St. Xavier University's Field-Based Master's Program, Prospect Heights, Illinois.

Figure 4.3c

Directed Reading-Thinking Activity

The Directed Reading-Thinking Activity, also known as the DRTA (Stauffer 1969), is a valuable activity that begins at the prereading stage and continues into the during reading stage until the topic "hooks" students so they proceed on their own. This strategy helps students realize that text is divided into segments, the completion of which can help them better understand the next segments. Students move through a selection by making predictions, reading to validate or reject the predictions made, making new predictions, and repeating the process. The predicting steps help students set a purpose for their reading while the validation/rejection process fosters purposeful reading. Finally, the entire procedure gives students an opportunity to practice their listening and speaking skills since they must reflect aloud and then justify their predictions (Richardson and Morgan 1997). Furthermore, once students become involved in the prediction process, they become motivated to read since, as in the Anticipation Guide strategy discussed previously, they are now reading to verify their own predictions not because the teacher told them to read!

 Steps for Directed Reading-Thinking Activity (DRTA)

While the DRTA is often used with narrative texts, it is equally effective with expository texts, which we focus on in this book.

1. Encourage students to activate their prior knowledge by previewing the chapter title, subtitles, charts, maps, pictures, and so on and sharing what they already know about the topic with the class.

2. Next, ask students to predict what information they think the author will cover in the chapter. Record these predictions on the board. For each prediction, ask the students to support their predictions by posing the question: Why do you think that? or Why is that a possibility? or What makes you think that?

3. Next, direct students to read a section of the chapter silently. After reading, ask students to support their answers by responding to Which predictions can you prove? Why or why not? so that they can confirm or reject their predictions.

4. Repeat this cycle until you feel the students can proceed on their own to complete the reading selection.

5. After the selection has been completed, you can extend learning by asking students to discuss their predictions, noting which needed revision and how they were revised. Be sure to ask students how their thinking was influenced by certain sentences or passages.

Sketch to Stretch

Sketch to Stretch (Harste, Short, and Burke 1988) is similar to the DRTA in that it also asks students to monitor their comprehension as they process what they are reading in sections. However, the richness in this strategy lies in the fact that it fosters students' listening skills while engaging their verbal/linguistic, visual/spatial, interpersonal, and intrapersonal intelligences. Teachers ask students to listen to a section of text and sketch what they visualize. Then the teacher distributes copies of the text to read and instructs students to revise their drawings to clarify details or to expand on the meaning after they read. Next, the students discuss what they have drawn with a peer and focus on what is important to remember from the text. We have adapted this strategy by adding another step. To extend learning, we ask students to reflect on which part of the process was most valuable in helping them understand what was heard or read.

 ### Steps for Sketch to Stretch

See Teacher Tips at the end of this chapter for a Blackline Master to use with this strategy (Figure 4.11).

1. Read the title of the selection out loud. Have students write what they already know about the topic in the Prediction box.

2. Instruct students to divide a sheet of paper into two boxes for each section to be read.

3. Read one section of the selection aloud and ask students to sketch (in the first box) what comes to mind as they listen.

4. After students complete their sketch, distribute copies of the text for students to read.

5. Advise students to revise the drawings by adding details.

6. When their drawings are complete, ask students to pair off and talk about their sketches, explaining what they were thinking about as they drew. Tell pairs to come to a consensus on what is important to remember from the text they listened to and read.

7. Tell students to summarize these important facts in the second box next to the picture.

8. Repeat this sequence until you feel the students can proceed on their own to complete the reading selection with adequate understanding.

9. As a last step, ask students to identify what aspect of the strategy most contributed to their learning.

DURING READING STRATEGIES

During reading strategies are utilized to help students become active readers and to interact with their text as they read. Two major kinds of during reading strategies are Note Taking and Study Guides.

Note Taking

There are a myriad of ways students can take notes, but the types that are most successful depend on students being able to identify exactly which ideas are important in the text. Too often students are unable to do this and, as a result, simply take too many notes, causing them to go on information overload. Taking too many notes is as futile as asking students to simply reread text chapters before a test. In order to be successful, students must have read their content area texts, gleaned important concepts, and then encoded that information in their own words. Two ways to help students accomplish this task are the Main Idea I and Structured Note Taking.

Main Idea I

Christen (1987) notes that successful learners must be able to recognize key concepts (main ideas) and organize them into meaningful patterns. In other words, they must be able to locate, select, organize, and remember important information so that they will be able to retrieve it from their long-term memories when needed. An effective way to teach students to do this is the Main Idea I (Christen 1987). Students use a graphic organizer to list three levels of information: the topic, the main idea, and the details. Next, students record their information, limiting it to seven to nine main ideas around any one concept being learned. Then they add a one or two sentence summary of the main idea and develop a "teacher-like" main idea question that ties the whole concept together. Using this strategy helps students to recognize important information, process it, and then organize it into a meaningful pattern for later retrieval, all important steps in helping students learn in a brain-compatible way. In addition, this strategy not only fosters the verbal/linguistic and visual/spatial intelligences, but the logical/mathematical ones as well.

 Steps for Main Idea I

See Teacher Tips at the end of this chapter for a Blackline Master to use with this strategy (Figure 4.12).

1. Have students preview a chapter of text to determine the topic and record it in the upper half of the circle of the Main Idea I graphic

organizer. This previewing serves as a sort of mental warm-up for students, getting them ready to accept the material they will be learning.

2. Next, instruct students to read a section or several sections of the text to determine the main ideas of the passages read. This step helps students set a purpose for their reading while asking them to be actively involved as they read. Advise students that they should select **no more** than seven to nine main ideas since common knowledge about memory tells us that people can only store seven to nine chunks of information in short-term memory; the rest is "shoved out." This argues for careful teacher planning and guidance in helping students select those seven to nine concepts that are most crucial to understanding the material to be learned. *Note:* For each main idea selected, tell students to develop a Main Idea I organizer. Direct them to record the main idea in the bottom half of the circle.

3. Tell students to reread the passage and record important details that support each main idea, recording their findings in the portion of the graphic organizer labeled *details.* This step is very valuable since students are asked to revisit the text with a specific purpose in mind. Rereading a text helps bring clarity to the concepts first read. At this point, your students have recorded exactly what information they must learn. The next steps in the process help students process and file the information into their long-term memories for later retrieval.

4 Instruct students to write one or two sentences that summarize the information for each main idea and record it directly under the Main Idea I graphic organizer. This step encourages students to actively process what they have just learned, and the act of writing it down in their own words helps cement the information into their long-term memory.

5. Finally, have students create a "teacher-like" main idea question that resembles a question they might see on a test about the material they are studying. Strategic readers constantly interact with the text, asking questions as they read. This process helps students to clarify and thus better understand what they are reading. Encouraging students to do this will help make them more strategic readers. Remind students to write questions at several levels: literal, inferential, evaluative, and applied.

Once students have mastered the Main Idea I method of note taking, the process can easily be transferred to other common forms of note taking such as mapping or two-column note taking.

Figure 4.4 shows how this strategy can be used with social studies.

Main Idea I for Social Studies

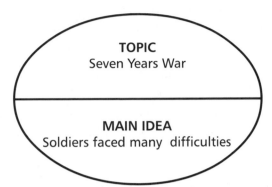

TOPIC
Seven Years War

MAIN IDEA
Soldiers faced many difficulties

QUESTION:
What difficulties did the soldiers face during the Seven Years War?

DETAILS

1. Much spoiled food so many became sick

2. Poor food supplies

3. Camps overcrowded and diseases, like typhoid fever, spread quickly

4. Most soldiers had little military experience so they didn't know how to fight well

SUMMARY: Soldiers faced many difficulties fighting in the Seven Years War.

Developed by Sandra Giangrasso, St. Xavier University's Field-Based Master's Program, Hanover Park, Illinois.

re 4.4

Structured Note Taking

Structured Note Taking (Smith and Tompkins 1988) is another effective way of helping students determine what information is important to take notes on. In addition, this strategy makes use of graphic organizers to help students visualize the information they are recording, thus clarifying the relationships among ideas for them. The richest aspect of Structured Note Taking, however, is that it helps students learn organizational patterns since the graphic organizer represents the reading selection's major text patterns.

Steps for Structured Note Taking

1. To better assist your students, preview the selection to be read to determine the organizational pattern used to convey the information. (See chapter 1 for common organizational patterns and questions that can be used to guide student reading.)

2. Next, create a graphic organizer that follows this pattern, complete with focusing questions, and distribute it as a study guide.

3. Instruct students to read the chapter and take notes by recording the appropriate information in the graphic organizer sections.

As time goes on, students will become adroit at spotting text organizational patterns and will be able to construct their own graphic organizers. Furthermore, by using graphic organizers developed according to the organizational pattern of the text, students can foster their logical/mathematic, visual/spatial, and verbal/linguistic intelligences.

Fig. 4.5a shows how this strategy can be used for health class; Figure 4.5b shows how it can be used for science class.

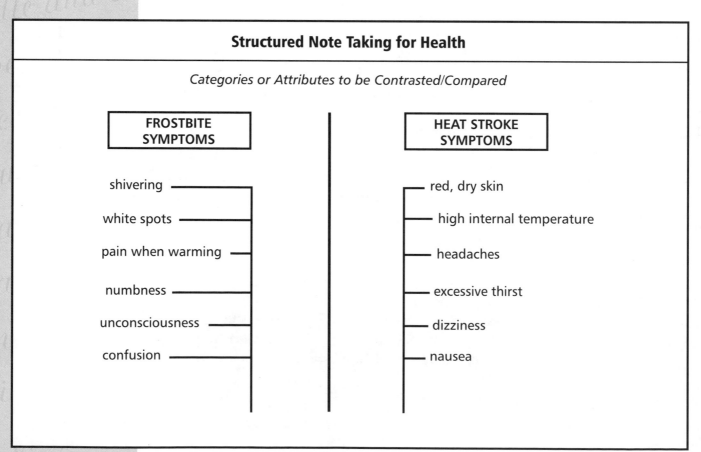

Figure 4.5a

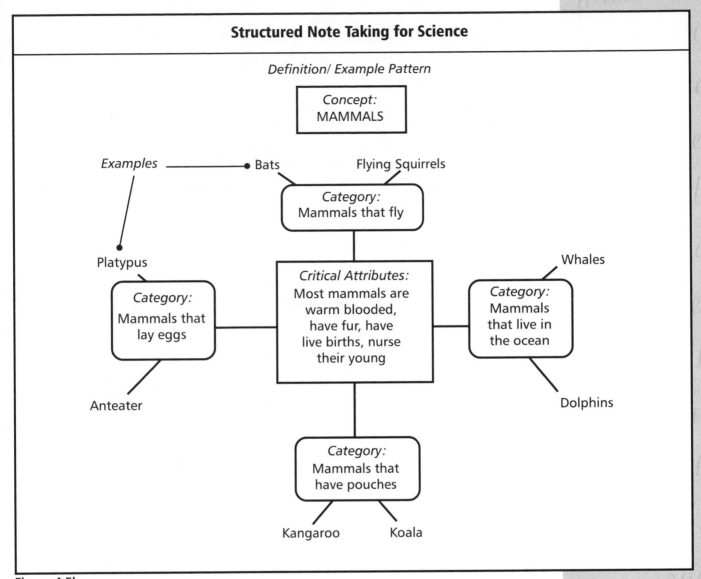

Structured Note Taking for Science

Definition/ Example Pattern

Concept:
MAMMALS

Examples — Bats

Flying Squirrels

Category:
Mammals that fly

Platypus

Whales

Category:
Mammals that
lay eggs

Critical Attributes:
Most mammals are
warm blooded,
have fur, have
live births, nurse
their young

Category:
Mammals
that live in
the ocean

Anteater

Dolphins

Category:
Mammals that
have pouches

Kangaroo   Koala

Figure 4.5b

Study/Reading Guides

Another effective during reading strategy is asking students to complete study or reading guides as they read. Study/Reading Guides differ from merely asking students to read the text and answer the questions at the end of the chapter. First, teachers develop Study/Reading Guides to help students focus their attention on the major concepts in a text chapter. As a result, students record information that is important rather than extraneous or irrelevant. Secondly, Study/Reading Guides promote active reading since students complete them as they read, rather than after they read. Wood and Mateja (1983) refer to Study/Reading Guides as print tutors.

While there are a myriad of Study/Reading Guides available, in our experience, two guides seem to be especially effective for use in content area classrooms: Three Level Guides and Point of View Study Guides.

Three Level Guide

The Three Level Guide (Herber 1978) is an excellent activity to help students become aware of the three levels of comprehension: literal, inferential, and applied. At the literal level, students simply identify the important information in the text or "get the author's message." Although this sounds like an easy task, not all readers are mature or strategic enough to accomplish this feat, and they may need guidance and practice in identifying and answering literal level questions. While it is important to be able to identify important information, strategic readers need to ferret out the author's intended meaning as well. They need to be able to read between the lines, make inferences, and draw conclusions; this is inferential reading. Finally, strategic readers must be able to realize the significance or importance of what is being read and consider how it can be applied to life situations. In other words, they must be able to apply what they have read; they need to be able to read at the applied level of comprehension. Teaching students to use the Three Level Guide fosters all these levels of comprehension.

 ### Steps for a Three Level Guide

1. Consider what specific ideas, concepts, and interpretations you want students to learn from the text. As you construct this list, focus on statements that reflect the author's intended or inferred meaning. Develop a series of five to six statements from your list; this is level two, the inferential level of your guide. Richardson and Morgan (1997) suggest that teachers may preface statements in this level of the guide with "The author means . . ."

2. Next, examine the inference statements you developed for level two and determine what explicit facts are needed to support them. Write these as statements for level one of the study guide. Richardson and Morgan (1997) note that often teachers will preface these statements with "The author says . . ." There should be at least two literal statements to support each major inference.

3. To develop level three, the applied level, construct four to five statements that help students connect prior knowledge to what they have learned. In this section, you want your students to actually apply their new knowledge in some fashion. Richardson and Morgan (1997) explain that these statements can be prefaced with "We can use . . ."

4. Finally, Vacca and Vacca (1996) suggest that in order to keep students focused as they read, you add distractors or a misleading fact to levels one and two to discourage students from marking items indiscriminately.

The Three Level Study Guide is a very effective strategy. However, when first using it with students you should model the strategy as a whole class activity. Later, students can do it independently and as a homework assignment. Finally, be careful not to overuse this strategy guide. Not every assignment lends itself to this type of study guide, and any strategy used again and again can become boring.

Figure 4.6a shows how the Three Level Study Guide can be used with science; Figure 4.6b shows how it can be used with social studies.

Three Level Study Guide for Science

Baffling Bats

Read pages 127–137 in your textbook. After reading, consider the statements below and place a + in the space next to each statement about bats you think is correct, true, or with which you agree based on what you have read. You will be asked to justify your answers in a class discussion so be sure to locate information from the text to support your answers.

LEVEL I
1. _____ Bats are scary and creepy creatures.
2. _____ Bats and birds are close relatives.
3. _____ Bats can eat 500 insects in an hour.
4. _____ Bats are smart enough to be trained like a dog.
5. _____ There are thirty-nine species of bats in the United States.

LEVEL II
1. _____ Bats cannot fly in the daytime.
2. _____ All bats are dangerous.
3. _____ Bats live in many different places.
4. _____ Bats have arms and fingers and even thumbs!
5. _____ Bats live very short lives.

LEVEL III
1. _____ People should protect bats rather than kill them.
2. _____ Bats help plants grow.
3. _____ Currently some bats in the United States are in danger of becoming extinct.
4. _____ Bats help our environment.
5. _____ We should protect bats so they do not become extinct.

Figure 4.6a

Three Level Study Guide for Social Studies

The Ancient Greeks and Romans

Read pages 24–38 in your textbook. On the basis of what you read, check the statements you think the author would agree with.

1. _____ The Romans were very practical people.
2. _____ Athens was a more civilized society than Sparta.
3. _____ Greeks were more skilled in government than Romans.
4. _____ Greece was conquered because people concentrated on art and literature instead of preparing themselves for war.
5. _____ Spartans felt that all people should be free.

Check the statements below that you would agree with based on what you have read.

1. _____ People form cities out of a common need.
2. _____ It is natural for humans to fight each other, even if they come from the same country or culture.
3. _____ The cultures of ancient Greece and Rome have influenced our present society.
4. _____ A leader is able to influence his followers both for good and for evil.
5. _____ During war, both sides in the battles suffer.

Check the statements below that you think are true based on what you know or feel; be prepared to defend your choices.

1. _____ The United States is a fair nation.
2. _____ The United States should mind its own business and never get involved in wars in other countries.
3. _____ It is the duty of the United States to keep peace in the world.
4. _____ It is the duty of the United States to take in all immigrants who come to our shores.
5. _____ Because of the wealth and power of the United States, it is our duty to provide resources to help other countries become rich and powerful, too.

Figure 4.6b

Point of View Study Guide

Another effective study guide is the Point of View Study Guide (Wood 1988), which asks students to assume a role as they read the text. This allows students to gain a different perspective on the reading topic while they enhance their ability to recall and comprehend the information read. In addition, it encourages them to elaborate on the topic by utilizing their prior knowledge. It allows students to put newly acquired information into their own words while learning the content of the selection (Wood, Lapp, and Flood 1992). This strategy follows an interview format by encouraging students to answer the interview questions in their own words, but from the perspective of their assumed roles.

Steps for Point of View Study Guide

1. Choose a piece of text and brainstorm with the class about a variety of perspectives from which it could be read. For example, in reading a selection on AIDS, students could assume the following perspectives: an AIDS victim, a relative of an AIDS victim, the AIDS virus, a doctor treating an AIDS victim, a boyfriend or girlfriend of an AIDS victim, or a medicine used to treat an AIDS victim.

2. Next, create a series of interview questions that focus on the major content information in the selection.

3. Then instruct students to read the text, locating information to answer the interview questions.

4. When students are ready to answer the interview questions, tell them to respond in the first person dialogue format and elaborate as much as they can with information from their personal experience.

This is an exciting activity for students since they are able to become personally involved in the procedure. As an added bonus, students can dress up as characters in the roles they have assumed and act out the interview. Thus, the multiple intelligences of bodily/kinesthetic and visual/spatial are fostered in addition to the verbal/linguistic.

Check out Figure 4.7a to see how the Point of View Study Guide can be used for health; see how it is used for mathematics in Figure 4.7b.

Point of View Study Guide for Health

Interview with a Microbe

Directions: You are about to be interviewed as if you were a microbe. As you watch the video Mystifying, Marvelous Microbes, answer the questions below as if you were a microbe.

1. I understand you are a microbe; exactly what is a microbe?

2. I know there are different types of microbes, but exactly how many are there?

3. What are the names of each of these microbes?

4. To help me get a clear idea of each type of microbe, would you please draw me a picture of each different type?

5. Where do these microbes live?

6. How big are the microbes?

7. Since microbes are so small, how do they draw attention to themselves?

8. How are microbes good for humans?

9. How are microbes bad for humans?

10. How can we prevent microbes from harming us?

Figure 4.7a

Point of View Study Guide for Mathematics

You are about to be interviewed as if you were a number from the Factor Multiple unit we are studying. Respond to the following questions as if you were a **Factor Tree.**

1. What number are you a factor tree for?
2. I notice that each branch of your tree holds all the factors of this number. Is this always necessary?
3. The bottom row of your tree seems to be all prime numbers. Could you please take a moment of your time to explain what this means?
4. Someone told me that this bottom row has a special name for itself. Do you know anything about this? Please explain it to me.

Thanks for your time.
This has been a great interview!

Developed by Diane Wilken, St. Xavier University's Field-Based Master's Program, Hanover Park, Illinois.

Figure 4.7b

AFTER READING STRATEGIES

While many teachers enrich their students' learning by using *prereading* and *during reading* strategies, far fewer engage students in *after reading* activities. However, after reading activities serve a definite purpose because they encourage students to think about, reflect on, apply, and sometimes even act upon the knowledge they have learned from their reading. In order to accomplish such action, after reading activities should be varied in nature so students can apply their reading, writing, listening, and speaking skills. The after reading strategies provided help students to comprehend and interact with the materials they have read.

Cubing

Cubing, first developed by Cowan and Cowan in 1980, encourages students to look at a topic from various aspects while using their writing and speaking skills to demonstrate knowledge. Vaughan and Estes (1986), propose that students can use the Cubing strategy to improve reading comprehension. For best results, ask students to think of a six-sided cube upon whose sides are written: Describe It; Compare It; Associate It; Analyze It; Apply It; and Argue For Or Against It. Then ask them to consider the topic they have studied from these perspectives. These six terms then provide a springboard for writing about or discussing an aspect of the topic just studied.

Steps for Cubing

1. Introduce the topic.
2. Give students five minutes to consider each side of the cube.
3. Ask them to talk or write about the topic from any one of the six possible aspects.

Perspective Cubing

Perspective Cubing (Whitehead 1994) utilizes a twist on the original cubing strategy by asking students to consider a graphic such as a map, chart, graph, or picture and reflect on it from the following perspectives: space, time, location, culture, talk, and size.

 Steps for Perspective Cubing

Here is a sample activity that can easily be adapted to different subjects and different grade levels.

1. Provide students with a copy of a map. Choose a location or an element of the map such as a river, mountain range, city, village, railroad track, park, or public building. (Your choice should be guided by the content to be studied. For example, if your class is studying the agriculture of Mexico in a geography class, you might focus on the Sierra Madre Mountain Range; if your class is studying the effects of immigration in social studies, you might focus on the banks of the Rio Grande River where illegal immigration is rampant.)

2. Then, ask students to consider the Sierra Madres or the Rio Grande from the perspectives of space, time, location, culture, talk, and size.

EXAMPLE OF PERSPECTIVE CUBING

SPACE

A. Sierra Madre Mountain Range

1. What do you think the mountain range looks like as you stand on it? What do you see from where you are?
2. What does it look like from far away? What can you see? Is it large? Small? Hidden in clouds?

B. Rio Grande River

1. What do you think the river looks like up close? What do you see if you stand in it?

2. What surrounds it?

TIME

A. Sierra Madre Mountain Range

1. What do we know about this mountain range today?

2. What do we think about it today?

3. Pretend this is 500 years in the future. Is the range still here? What does it look like now? How has it changed? What is its importance?

B. Rio Grande River

1. What do we know about this river today?

2. What do we think about it today?

3. Pretend this is 100 years in the future. Is the river still here? What does it look like now? How has it changed? What is its importance?

LOCATION

A. Sierra Madre Mountain Range

1. What does the mountain range look like from above? From the side? From below?

2. Describe the physical characteristics you can see from each of these different vantage points.

B. Rio Grande River

1. What does the river look like from above? From the side? From below?

2. Describe the physical characteristics you can see from each of these different vantage points.

CULTURE

A. Sierra Madre Mountain Range

1. What do the citizens of Guadalajara think of this mountain range? What do the citizens of Puerto Vallarata think of this mountain range? What do the citizens of the rest of Mexico think of this mountain range?

2. What do the citizens of the United States think of this mountain range?

3. What do vacationers or travel agents think of this mountain range?

4. What do the citizens of Europe think of this mountain range?

5. What might the first inhabitants (Indians) have thought of this mountain range?

B. Rio Grande River

1. What do the citizens of Laredo, Texas, think of this river?
2. What do immigration officers think of this river?
3. What do the citizens of Nueva Laredo, Mexico, think of this river?
4. What do vacationers or travel agents think of this river?
5. What do the citizens of Europe think of this river?
6. What might the first inhabitants (Indians) have thought of this river?

TALK

A. Sierra Madre Mountain Range

1. If this mountain range could talk, what story would it tell?
2. Who would it tell its story to?

B. Rio Grande River

1. If this river could talk, what story would it tell?
2. Who would it tell its story to?

SIZE

A. Sierra Madre Mountain Range

1. If this mountain range could change size, would it get larger, smaller, taller, or shorter?
2. How would its change in size affect our thoughts about it?

B. Rio Grande River

1. If this river could change size, would it get longer, shorter, deeper, or more shallow?
2. How would its change in size affect our thoughts about it?

Both Cubing and Perspective Cubing appeal to students' creativity and allow them to demonstrate their knowledge from a variety of perspectives. Since the responses can be either oral or written and done individually or in a small group, students utilize verbal/linguistic, visual/spatial, intrapersonal, and interpersonal intelligences. See Figure 4.8 for topic ideas across content areas.

Suggestions for Cubing and Perspective Cubing Topics					
Social Studies	**Mathematics**	**Science**	**Business**	**Health/PE**	**Fine Arts**
Manifest Destiny	prime numbers	diffusion	cost effectiveness	AIDS	allegro
democracy	equation	osmosis	budget	respiration	impressionism
fascism	polynomial	nucleus	cut backs	digestion	sonata
isolationism	factor	evolution	monopoly	immunity	etching
communism	simplify	photosynthesis	surplus	contagion	shading

Figure 4.8

Magnet Summaries

Summaries, as we know, are merely brief statements that contain the essential ideas from longer passages or selections. While this sounds like a simple task, as teachers we know that writing a summary is often not a simple task at all. In fact, in working with academically challenged students, we have discovered that the greatest challenge they have is deciding which details are important and which can be eliminated. An excellent after reading strategy that encourages summarizing while improving students' writing skills is Magnet Summaries (Buehl 1995). In order to complete the Magnet Summaries strategy, students must first identify keywords from the passages read. Once these keywords have been determined, the students use them to develop a summary of the passage.

 Steps for a Magnet Summary

See Teacher Tips at the end of this chapter for a Blackline Master to use with this strategy (Figure 4.13).

1. After assigning a passage to be read, help students determine some keywords from the passage. Keywords relate directly to the concept being taught.
2. Explain to students that these keywords are like magnets in that they attract information that is important to the topic.
3. Next, ask students to recall details from the passage that are connected to the magnet words. Both the word and the details should be recorded on a 3×5 index card.
4. After students have recorded their magnet words and supporting details on cards, show them how the information can be developed into a short summary. Strive to have students develop a one-sentence summary whenever possible.

5. Once all the cards have been summarized, ask students to arrange their sentences in logical order to develop a coherent summary. Remind students that they may have to edit sentences so their summaries will flow smoothly.

The Magnet Summaries strategy provides many advantages as an after reading strategy. While it gives students practice in expressing key concepts in their own words, its greatest value lies in providing a logical and simple procedure for helping students determine relevant and irrelevant details as they synthesize the information. While this strategy appears simple, its success depends on teacher modeling to guide students through the process before they produce Magnet Summaries independently. See Figure 4.9 for an example of Magnet Summaries.

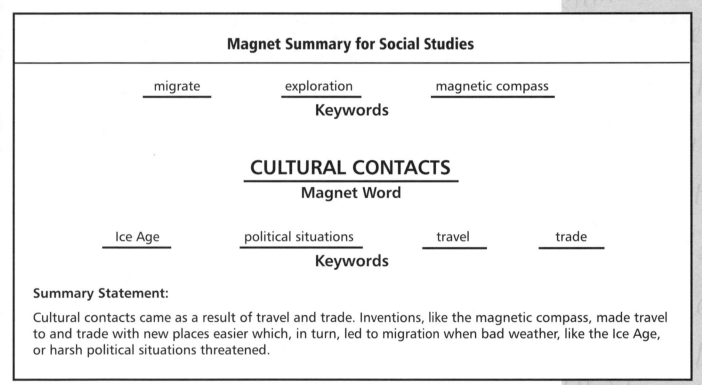

Magnet Summary for Social Studies

| migrate | exploration | magnetic compass |

Keywords

CULTURAL CONTACTS
Magnet Word

| Ice Age | political situations | travel | trade |

Keywords

Summary Statement:

Cultural contacts came as a result of travel and trade. Inventions, like the magnetic compass, made travel to and trade with new places easier which, in turn, led to migration when bad weather, like the Ice Age, or harsh political situations threatened.

Figure 4.9

Socratic Questioning

A very effective after reading strategy that asks students to utilize their listening and speaking skills is Socratic Questioning. As classroom teachers we are, perhaps, familiar with Sir Francis Bacon's wise words, "Reading maketh a full man; conference a ready man; and writing an exact man." Yet how often do we successfully engage students in conference? For most students, classroom discussions are a time to answer the teacher's questions with a brief response. Often these discussions are not a time to delve into, reflect upon, and extend the concepts presented in the question in a lively, animated, high level conversation. This, however, is exactly what we need to encourage our students to do; they need to learn to ask why, to explore their own personal beliefs about a concept, and to listen, analyze, and reflect upon what others say about that concept and respond. The Socratic Dialogue strategy, which is based on Socrates' belief that students must learn to think for themselves rather than just get the right answer, encourages critical thinking.

 ### *Steps for Socratic Questioning*

1. Students read a text, rich in ideas, issues, and values, which will stimulate thought and dialogue.

2. After reading, the dialogue is opened with a question, which may be posed by the leader or any of the participants. This question has no "official" correct answer but, instead, leads the students into thoughtful reflection and new questions.

3. The success of the discussion depends on the students' abilities to read analytically, listen carefully, reflect on the questions asked, and ask critical, thought-provoking questions in response.

EXAMPLE OF SOCRATIC QUESTIONING

Fogarty (1997) provides an extensive list of questions that are effective in Socratic Questioning.

What reasons do you have for saying that?

Why do you agree or disagree with that point?

How are you defining the term?

What do you mean by that expression?

Is what you're saying now consistent with what you said before?

Could you clarify that comment?

When you said that, what was implied by your remarks?

What follows from what you just said?

Is it possible that you are contradicting each other?

Could you clarify that remark?

Are you sure that you are not contradicting yourself?

What alternatives are there?

Could you give an example of that?

Are you familiar with incidents of this sort?

Why did you find that interesting?

Are you saying . . . ?

I wonder if what you're saying is . . . ?

So, you see it as . . . ?

Is that the point you're making?

Can I sum up what you've said by . . . ?

Are you suggesting . . . ?

If you're correct, would it follow . . . ?

The implications of what you've said seem far reaching if . . . then . . . ?

Aren't you assuming . . . ?

Is what you've just said based on . . . ?

What is your reason for saying that . . . ?

Why do you believe . . . ?

What can you say in defense of that view?

How do you know?

Couldn't it also be . . . ?

What if someone . . . ?

From *Brain-Compatible Classrooms* by Robin Fogarty. © 1997 SkyLight Training and Publishing, Inc. Reprinted by permission of SkyLight Professional Development.

CHAPTER SUMMARY

Chapter 4 discusses the importance of teaching students how to read strategically by using the process approach. Several strategies that help students become more successful before they read, while they read, and after they have finished the text are presented.

COMPUTER CONNECTIONS

1. As a review procedure, place students in groups of three and assign them a section of the chapter to read. After reading the section, have students practice the Structured Note Taking strategy by identifying the pattern of organization used to construct the passage and then developing a graphic organizer to match that pattern. Finally, students create the graphic organizer on the computer and flesh it out with details from the section read. The completed organizer is then printed out as an overhead transparency, and each group presents their organizer to the class in a "student as teacher" format to highlight the important points of the chapter.

2. Assign students partners. Then, individually, have each partner create a Three Level Study Guide for a section of the chapter assigned by the teacher. The guides should be created as an e-mail file, and, when completed, the e-mail is sent to the student's partner. Each partner then completes the Three Level Guide sent to him or her and e-mails the answers back to the partner for evaluation. As an alternative, each student can be assigned a different section of the chapter and can e-mail the Three Level Guides to the teacher or other members of the class in a round-robin format.

3. Place students in groups and assign them a section of the chapter to read. When they have completed the section, ask them to create a Magnet Summary to summarize the important points of the chapter. These Magnet Summaries can be typed using the computer and then printed out and compiled for use as a review of the chapter.

Teacher Tips

❶ Have students brainstorm different points of view that can be taken when reading a textbook selection. Make a collection of these differing viewpoints to use when assigning the Point of View Study Guide strategy for students to complete.

❷ Use the Blackline Masters provided for the following strategies:

   a. Knowledge Rating (Figure 4.10)

   b. Organizer for Sketch to Stretch (Figure 4.11)

   c. Main Idea I (Figure 4.12)

   d. Magnet Summary (Figure 4.13)

Knowledge Rating

Directions: In the space provided, write the words your teacher has chosen. Respond individually to each category by placing an X in the appropriate boxes. Be ready to explain or illustrate your responses.

Word	Have Seen or Heard	Can Say	Can Define	Can Spell	Can Use in a Sentence	Don't Know at All

Based on Blachowicz 1991

Figure 4.10

Organizer for Sketch to Stretch

Directions: Listen as your teacher reads the title of the selection. Think of what you already know about the topic you will be reading about. Write about it in the section entitled Prediction. Next, listen as your teacher reads a section of text aloud. Sketch what comes to mind as you listen. After you complete your sketch, you will receive a copy of the text to read. You can revise the drawings by adding details. Then, you can pair off with a classmate and talk about your sketches, explaining what you were thinking about as you drew. Arrive at a consensus about what is important to remember from the text you listened to and read. Summarize these important facts in the box next to the picture.

Prediction:

Sketch	Summary of Important Points
Sketch	Summary of Important Points
Sketch	Summary of Important Points

Figure 4.11

Main Idea I

Directions: Preview a chapter of text to determine the topic and record it in the space provided. Then, read a section to determine the main idea. Reread the passage, and record important details that support each main idea. Record your findings in the portion of the graphic organizer labeled details. Write one or two sentences that summarize the information for each main idea and record it in the appropriate section. Finally, create a "teacher-like" main idea question that you might see on a test about the material you are studying. Write questions at several levels: literal, inferential, evaluative, and applied.

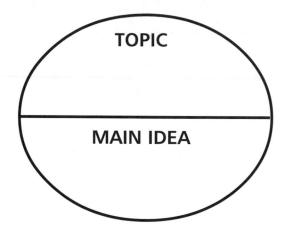

QUESTIONS:

DETAILS

SUMMARY:

Based on Christen 1987

Figure 4.12

Magnet Summary

Directions: Select a keyword from the passage. Write the keyword (Magnet Word) in the middle of the card and record pertinent details at the top and bottom of the card. Finally, write a summary statement in the space provided.

_____ _____ _____ _____ _____

Keywords

_____

Magnet Word

_____ _____ _____ _____ _____

Keywords

Summary Statement:

Figure 4.13

Research Writing

Clear thinking becomes clear writing; one can't exist without the other.

William Zinsser

Creating the
Framework
for Reading

Setting the
Framework
for Writing

Keying into
Vocabulary

Strategies for
Comprehension

**Research
Writing**

Integrating
Reading and
Writing in
the Classroom

Assessing
Reading
and Writing

NONTRADITIONAL RESEARCH

From the time children can talk, they are curious enough to search for answers to their questions. They want to know where their teddy bear is, why they have to eat vegetables, and whether or not they can go to the park. When they do not get satisfactory answers to their questions, they will search for another answer by asking, But why?

Elementary School

As children's horizons broaden and they go off to school, their need to know answers increases. Elementary school teachers provide the basic tools to help them find answers and to distinguish between facts and opinions. In addition, they often provide activities that foster research, as in the following examples using a primary resource.

Most children know the story of *Cinderella*. Teachers can use the KWL technique, discussed in detail in chapter 6, to discover what details students remember. Then, teachers can read the story and ask the students to record key points in the appropriate column on a ready-made chart. Next, teachers can read two or three different versions of the same tale and record the similar features on the chart. Teachers can use the chart to discuss the similarities and differences in the tale, and they can use it as a springboard for writing. Teachers in other content areas can use primary sources like letters, documents, and notes to discuss and draw similarities in styles, backgrounds, policies, and ideas of the authors (see Figure 5.1).

Cinderella

Directions: Use the headings at the top of the chart to identify the features in three different versions of a familiar story.

Author & Title	Setting	Characters	Dress	Conflict	Resolution

Figure 5.1

Teachers at this level also teach students how to use secondary sources. Notice how the following example combines research with a hands-on approach.

> Children often help their parents when they see them planting a garden; therefore, creating a small vegetable garden in a classroom setting should not be too difficult. First, have the class create a list of things they need to buy; then have them list things they need to do so their vegetables will grow. Next, read a textbook that explains how to grow a particular kind of vegetable. Have students list the steps that the book describes and then compare them with their original list, adding elements as needed. Finally, gather the materials and have students keep journals that track the progress of their vegetable. As a culminating activity, teachers can use the journals for reflection and discussion or to connect to other activities within the curriculum.

By the time students enter the fourth grade, teachers want them to be able to go beyond the literal level of reading comprehension. In addition, they require their students to read information from many different kinds of books, including reference books.

Middle School

Most students must complete at least one research assignment in middle school. The process can be a simple one where they only have to check one or two sources to find the answer; or, it can be more complex, where they must look at several sources and document them.

Many parents can relate stories about helping their middle school child with the dreaded science fair project. Sharon Thiese remembers when her son collected different kinds of soil to test plant growth, when he tried to grow mold, and the time he and his dad tried to build a battery to conduct electricity. In spite of the fact that these projects caused everyone frustration, they did help her son learn how to do research and how to solve problems.

Students at this level are usually required to complete an in-depth research assignment and to draw conclusions about it. For example, in social studies, students could research the significance of Paul Revere's ride; in mathematics, they could research one or more theories in geometry and determine their usefulness in building design today; in music, they could research the works of a particular composer to discover which one had the greatest influence on society and why; and in science, they could compare and contrast two different islands to determine which provided the best living conditions. (See example in Figure 5.2.)

Middle School Example

Assignment:

Use the chart below to identify the contrasting features of two islands. Once you have completed the research, determine which island offers a better environment or a better economy and present your findings to the class.

Example:

Bahamas	Features	Sanibel Island
	Size	
	Land features	
	Bodies of water	
	Climate	
	Natural resources	
	Animals	
	Commerce and trade	
	Population characteristics	
	Government	
	Education	

Figure 5.2

High School

Once students reach high school, they are often required to complete several research projects and/or papers at the same time. Many teachers prefer to assign research projects because they provide their students with more variety and use a less structured approach.

Frequently, these assignments may be quite sophisticated, so students need to revise their notes to fit the format of the assignment. For example, in science, students might have to discover how and why a particular species of animal became endangered, and what scientists are doing to protect the species now. They could be required to present their information in a Power Point presentation. In social studies, students might have to research the monuments in a particular state and determine which one is most significant to the public and why. They could be required to present this information in the form of a pamphlet or a video presentation.

Newspaper Project

In English, students might use Sharon Thiese's newspaper project, which asks the students to interview an older person, preferably a family member: a great grandparent, grandparent, or an older aunt or uncle. If they do not have an older extended relative, they can choose an older friend of the family.

The goal of the project is for them to find some background information about their interviewee's past and about the time period in which he or she lived. While the interview is used as a primary resource, students must also read several

I turned in my semester research project today! I copied from at least five volumes of our encyclopedia last night.

secondary sources and taking notes in order to complete the final product: a newspaper publication. The newspaper should represent significant experiences, accomplishments, and beliefs of the interviewee, as well as information about the time period. See Figure 5.3 for an example of teacher guidelines, Figure 5.4 for the newspaper project checklist, Figure 5.5 for a sample menu of activities, and Figure 5.6 for sample grading criteria (rubric). Refer to Teacher Tips at the end of this chapter for convenient Blackline Masters of the Newspaper Research Project: Student Guidelines Checklist and the Menu of Activities for Newspaper Research Project (Figures 5.16 and 5.17).

Newspaper Research Project: Teacher Guidelines

Follow these procedures to help students achieve success on this research project.

Steps:

1. Early in the school year, set up the scenario that students are meeting each other for the first time. Tell them to brainstorm a list of questions they can ask each other; however, they may not use simple yes or no questions. Record the questions on the chalkboard or overhead.

2. Pair up students and tell them to interview each other. The purpose of the interview is to get in-depth information about one part of the student's life. Students may need to create another list of questions to complete this focused interview. Tell them to record their answers as they interview each other.

3. Students use their interview and rewrite it in a journal form. They must include a quote.

4. Repeat this procedure using other formats like responding to a text to give students practice for this part of their research project.

5. As you introduce the research assignment, provide some time to let the students browse through modern newspapers. Point out the different styles of writing. Let small groups practice writing different forms and share them with the class.

6. Set aside one day for students to bring in one or more of their secondary sources. Teach them how to write note cards, bibliography cards, and a bibliography.

7. Make a transparency of the menu of activities to use as you explain the project.

8. Make a calendar with due dates for the students.

9. Review the grading guides with the students.

10. Allow time for students to use the computer lab, particularly if you have a publisher's program.

11. Provide individual conference time as needed.

12. Provide a checklist for the project.

Figure 5.3

Newspaper Project Checklist

Teachers and/or students can use the following checklist as they complete the research project.

Student_____

Assignment	Completed
Interview a family member.	
Remember to focus on a specific time period.	
Choose activities from the menu of activities.	
All students complete #1 and #9 and choose one 20-point activity and choose three 16-point activities from the Menu of Activities for the Newspaper Research Project.	
Keep notes from your interview.	
Take notes on index cards as you read secondary sources.	
Keep track of the bibliographical information on index cards.	
Use your notes to create the newspaper.	
Follow the grading criteria for both parts of the project.	
Follow the calendar to meet all due dates.	

Figure 5.4

Sample Menu of Activities for Newspaper Research Project

Directions: Have students circle their choices.
Guidelines:
1. Everyone must complete #1 (people profile) and #9 (personal profile) from the menu.
2. Choose **one** 20-point activity: #5 (editorial) or #7 (home life).
3. Choose **three** 16-point activities: #2 (travel), #3 (obituary), #4 (entertainment), #6 (advice column), and #8 (classified ads).

1	**2**	**3**
People Profile	**Travel**	**Obituary**
Focused journal or news story (interview); 1 page; include a quote.	Create a map of person's birthplace. Include: state, city, or town of birthplace; topographic features; key points of interest; and population. Use closest time period and five descriptors that relate to person.	Write about a significant but less well-known person from the town or state and from the time period.
20 pts	**16 pts**	**16 pts**
4	**5**	**6**
Entertainment	**Editorial**	**Advice Column**
Create an advertisement for sports event, book, musician, artist, exhibit, etc. from the time period.	Write a letter to the editor voicing your opinion about an issue of the time period.	Write two letters to an advice columnist about problems of the time. Include answers.
16 pts	**20 pts**	**16 pts**
7	**8**	**9**
Home Life	**Classified**	**Personal Profile**
Write a news story or two comic strips about the customs or traditions of the time.	Create three ads for one of the following: help wanted or real estate of time period.	Write a focused journal or a profile explaining how you are like the interviewee.
20 pts	**16 pts**	**16 pts**

Figure 5.5

English I Honors

Name _____

Sample Research Project: Grading Criteria—Newspaper Format

Directions: Students should circle their choices where indicated in the first column.

Criteria	1	2	3	4	Score
People Profile • focus on 1 area • description and details reveal person's traits • quote 1 page • journal or news story	Incomplete in several areas	2 elements missing or 1 missing and 1 unclear	1 element missing or 1 unclear	All elements complete and clear	____ × 5 = _____

*Choose **One** of the Following:*

Criteria	1	2	3	4	Score
Editorial • letter to editor • identify issue/event of the time (who, what, when, where) • opinion • uses research	Incomplete in several areas	2 elements missing or 1 missing and 1 unclear	1 element missing or 1 unclear	All elements complete and clear	____ × 5 = _____
Home Life • custom/tradition of the time (who, what, when, where) • news story or 2 comics • uses research	Incomplete in several areas	2 elements missing or 1 missing and 1 unclear	1 element missing or 1 unclear	All elements complete and clear	____ × 5 = _____

*Choose **Three** of the Following:*

Criteria	1	2	3	4	Score
Travel • map of area and the time include topography, key points of interest, 5 descriptors that relate to person • color and label • uses research	Incomplete in several areas	2 elements missing or 1 missing and 1 unclear	1 element missing or 1 unclear	All elements complete and clear	____ × 4 = _____
Entertainment • create an ad for event of the time—use pictures and words (who, what, when, where) • uses research	Incomplete in several areas	2 elements missing or 1 missing and 1 unclear	1 element missing or 1 unclear	All elements complete and clear	____ × 4 = _____
Advice Column • write 2 letters to columnist about problem of the time • include answers • uses research	Incomplete in several areas	2 elements missing or 1 missing and 1 unclear	1 element missing or 1 unclear	All elements complete and clear	____ × 4 = _____

Figure 5.6 *(continues on next page)*

Research Project: Grading Criteria—Newspaper Format (continued)

Criteria	1	2	3	4	Score
Obituary • person from area • includes dates, family, accomplishments • uses research	Incomplete in several areas	2 elements missing or 1 missing and 1 unclear	1 element missing or 1 unclear	All elements complete and clear	_____ × 4 = _____
Classified • 3 ads from the time (help wanted, real estate) • pictures and words • uses research	Incomplete in several areas	2 elements missing or 1 missing and 1 unclear	1 element missing or 1 unclear	All elements complete and clear	_____ × 4 = _____
Personal Profile • compares self and interviewee • 1 page journal or 12 page profile	Incomplete in several areas	2 elements missing or 1 missing and 1 unclear	1 element missing or 1 unclear	All elements complete and clear	_____ × 4 = _____
Additional Grading Criteria					
Format • masthead • headlines • columns • legible	Incomplete in several areas	2 elements missing or 1 missing and 1 unclear	1 element missing or 1 unclear	All elements complete and clear	_____ × 2 = _____
Grammar • correct usage, spelling, etc.	6 or more errors	5 errors	4 errors	0–3 errors	_____ × 1 = _____

_____ / 100

Figure 5.6 (continued)

ALTERNATIVE RESEARCH

I-Search Project

Ken Macrorie (1988) provides an interesting alternative to the traditional method of research paper writing. In his I-Search procedure, students are invited to investigate a topic they are particularly interested in by doing some hands-on research. They might interview experts in the field or on the topic and visit places relevant to the topic. They then report on their research in a nontraditional manner that provides a sort of narrative to their research adventure.

Steps for I-Search

The basic I-Search procedures follow this format:

1. Students choose a topic that interests them.

2. Students formulate a plan of action to carry out their research. A major feature of this step is for students to figure out where they can find experts to interview. Students need to be encouraged to search for this expert among classmates, teachers, parents, and the community in which they live. Another aspect of this step is for students to do some background reading to create effective interview questions.

3. Students conduct the actual interview. Students need to be encouraged to record their interview in an appropriate fashion, be it by taking notes or by using a tape recorder or a video camera to record pertinent information.

4. During this step, students actually tell the story of their research project, making it as personal as possible by including information about why they chose their topic, what they learned about their topic, what special experiences they had as they did their research, and so forth.

5. The I-Search paper concludes with a list of sources as well as experts interviewed.

See Figure 5.7 for I-Search Project information. Also see Computer Connections at the end of this chapter for an adaptation of an I-Search Project (Figures 5.14 and 5.15).

See Figure 5.8 for a useful list of suggested topics. Also refer to Figure 5.14 to make use of the Criteria for I-Search Paper developed by Ann Kimpton and Marilyn Payton.

I-Search Project

Purpose: To gain an in-depth understanding of a particular issue and to form an opinion about that issue.

To understand the use of various sources for research.

To evaluate sources and information collected.

To create a bibliography.

To produce a pamphlet using a computer to support the opinion the researcher has formulated.

Resources: The researcher must use at least four resources.

I. **Required Sources**
   A. Book—You must use at least one book.
   B. Internet—You must use at least one Internet site.
   C. Interview—You must use at least one interview; however, this will count as one source, even if you do more than one interview.

II. **Optional Sources—at least one of the following must be used:**
   A. Reference Books—These will count as only one of four sources.
      1. Almanac—facts and statistics
      2. Atlas—maps and population
      3. Encyclopedia—general information on people, place, animals, and things
   B. Periodicals—These will count as only one of four sources.
      1. Magazines and newspapers—appropriate articles can be located on a computer program.
      2. Vertical file—pamphlets and news articles located in the library

III. **Students use the computer to prepare a trifold brochure to report their I-Search findings. They may use a comparison/contrast, cause/effect, or problem/solution format. (See chapters I and 2 for a discussion of these formats.)**

Figure 5.7

to make use of the Criteria for I-Search Paper developed by Ann Kimpton and Marilyn Payton.

Suggested Topics

When choosing a topic, it will be helpful to pick one in which you have an interest, but not a great deal of knowledge. Also remember that you must be able to formulate a question about which you can have an opinion that will be supported in your pamphlet.

Issues	Topics
Global Issues	World hunger Ecology Use of energy sources Garbage Cloning Biological or chemical warfare Nuclear waste Overpopulation Pollution—air, water, noise, etc. Rain forests Timber of the Northwest
Legal Issues	Gun control Crime and science (DNA testing, lie detectors, etc.) Crime prevention Rights of the accused—rights of victims Police brutality Sexual harassment Death penalty Euthanasia—assisted suicide Prayer in schools
Social Issues	Teens and sex—abstinence Divorce and its effects on families Teen pregnancy—teen fathers Child custody Dating violence—date rape Single parenting Homelessness Poverty Gambling Welfare—Who receives it? Why? Grief—coping with death Adoption rights—open vs. closed adoptions Lotteries Surrogate mothers
Alcohol and Drugs	Effects of drugs Alchoholism—causes, effects on drinkers, effects on families, etc. Drug abuse treatment Smoking Drug abuse prevention Drinking/smoking habits of teens—peer pressure
Prejudice and Discrimination	Prejudice—causes, effects, prevention Groups who have experienced discrimination: elderly; White supremacist groups disabled or mentally ill; poor; women; African- (e.g., Klu Klux Klan) Americans; Jews; Japanese (internment during World War II)
Health and Medicine	Eating disorders—anorexia or bulimia AIDS Fetal alcohol syndrome Body image Biomedical ethics Organ donation
Sports Issues	Cheating Recruitment of athletes Gender equity Violence in sports Drugs and sports (steroids) Science and sports performance
Media and Technology	Advertising Violence on television—programs, news What persuasion techniques do advertisers use? Values portrayed in television, in movies Alcohol advertising Television rating system Cigarette advertising Media and politics Should advertisements be aimed at kids? Internet—a positive or negative influence How technology has changed—how will it change Virtual reality and its uses
Educational Issues	Equal opportunity—gender, socioeconomic class, etc. Illiteracy Trends in education Learning disabilities—ADD Censorship in school, in libraries
Food	Fads, changes, nutritional information, and its effects on our eating habits Foods of different cultures How safe is our food? (food additives)
Miscellaneous	Immigration, past and present Illegal immigrants Animal welfare
Subjects to Avoid	ESP Deja vu Bermuda Triangle Psychics Satanic cults Life after death

Note: If you are interested in a topic not listed on this sheet, discuss it with your teacher.

Developed by Ann Kimpton and Marilyn Payton, Willowbrook High School, Villa Park.

Figure 5.8

RESEARCH SKILLS

Research skills are not easy to master at any level; in fact, many students find them tedious, because they need to complete a long list of requirements all at once. Therefore, it is important to have a reliable system in place that will help students meet the teacher's requirements. All students need to have a method for conducting their research and recording the results; they must be able to use the library effectively and to cite the origins of their sources properly.

Teachers often assume that students know how to use the library. This is not always the case; with more students using computers now, they may not even recognize the term *card (or online) catalog*, let alone know how to use it. It is a good idea for teachers to take the time to review some of the key resources in the library. They can do this by asking the librarians to give a book talk or by creating activities that will require students to use different reference sources. They might also create questions that relate to the sources in the library and use those sources in a library scavenger hunt activity or in a game to see who can answer the most items correctly. See Figure 5.9 for a Library Inventory.

THE RESEARCH PROCESS

A traditional approach to research often views the process in two parts: research and writing. In the first part of this process, students complete all of the research for the assignment, and then they sit down to write their papers. However, in order to help students cope with the complex tasks of researching, note taking, documentation, and writing, teachers need to create activities to guide students through each step of the research (Zemelman and Daniels 1988).

Planning

Teachers can help students plan for the research project by remembering a few basic points:

1. Clarify the project's requirements, which include: topic choice, source requirements, length and type of assignment, and a list of due dates for each part of the assignment.
2. Provide students time to consult and use library sources.
3. Create a checklist to keep track of student's progress for each step of this process. See the Teacher's Tips at the end of this chapter for Blackline Masters of the Traditional Research Process Approach and Checklist (Figures 5.18 and 5.19).

Library Inventory

How well do you know the library? See how many of the following questions you can answer.

1. What is a book of maps called?

2. Can you identify the title of the reference that helps you find magazine articles?

3. What book lists names of people in alphabetical order and gives facts about them?

4. Where can you find clippings of newspaper and magazine articles?

5. What publication lists charts and tables on various topics?

6. Can you name the file that gives the information of the author and title of a book?

7. Can you name the system that librarians use to classify books?

8. Can you name the reference that is a weekly world news digest?

9. What source would you consult to find general information about a subject?

10. What source would you consult to find information about someone famous who is still living?

Figure 5.9

Note Taking

Since note taking is an important part of reading and research, teachers need to decide which method(s) of note taking they want their students to use and to give their students practice using that method(s). Some common methods of note taking include:

1. Photocopy the originals or print them from a computer. Underline key ideas with a pen or a highlighter.
2. Use sticky notes to mark key passages.
3. List or outline key ideas and details.
4. Use index cards to keep track of the information.

Sharon Thiese requires freshmen to use index cards. She believes the cards help students organize their ideas more effectively. In addition, she thinks that the cards make it easier for students to move chunks of material and to write directly from the cards. Although she lets seniors use their own style of note taking, she teaches them different options of note taking and reviews the three ways to take notes: summary, paraphrasing, and quotations.

Documenting

Teachers should also have students practice documenting their sources. It is easy to practice this skill by providing models on an overhead or a handout, and to ask students to use their own resources, along with their grammar handbook, to complete a few examples in class. By giving students several opportunities to gather material from other sources and incorporate their ideas into writing, teachers lay the foundation for the traditional research paper.

TRADITIONAL RESEARCH

Writing a formal research paper is by no means an easy task. In fact, Sharon Thiese often hears seniors grumbling about the prospect of writing it as early as September, even though she does not assign the paper until the second semester. To make this task less complex, she uses the process approach to teach research.

Since her students are required to research a problem and discover several solutions for it, she begins the process by designing activities to explore topics. First, students work with a partner to identify five different problems; they are not allowed to research abortion, euthanasia, or the death penalty, since there are no clear-cut solutions to these problems. Next, they list all of the topics on the board. Partners choose one of the problems and identify the problem (what is it?) and give some general background information on the problem (who, what, when, where, and why) and the causes for it based on what they know. Then, they write their information on an index card. Volunteers share their information with the class. Students begin to understand the dimensions of identifying and exploring a problem at this point. They practice the same procedure to identify problems by watching clips from the news, looking at topics in newspapers and magazines, and by looking at subject headings in research guides. Once students understand this part of the process, they receive the guidelines and the grading criteria for each assignment along with a calendar of due dates.

 Steps for Research

1. Instruct students to choose a topic, find an article related to the topic, and bring the article to class.
2. Have students write a journal entry related to the newspaper article, which defines the problem and gives general background information about it based on what they know.
3. Ask students to rewrite the topic in the form of a question.

4. Have students write ten more questions about the topic.

5. Direct students to complete the following activities related to the topic:

    a. Describe the problem as they see it now.

    b. Define and/or identify key terms that are related to the problem.

    c. List some effects of the problem.

    d. Give the best solution as they see it now.

    e. Sketch an outline of their ideas.

    f. Revisit the solution to see if it needs to be changed.

    g. Sketch an outline of their ideas.

Do you think I can use one of the frogs as a primary resource for my paper?

6. Give students a day in the library where they must find three different sources to bring to class the next day. They learn different note taking skills and how to document their sources at this point.

7. Teach students how to write a thesis statement in class and create a working outline.

8. Have students submit a rough draft for each part of their papers and give them grading criteria for each part. These parts include: proof of the problem, three groups harmed or hurt, and three possible solutions.

9. The last part of the process is to teach students how to complete the title page, write the lead, the conclusion, and the Works Cited page.

10. Conference with each student so they know how to make revisions on their final papers.

Students write better research papers when they use the process method. They find it is easier to look for information, gather notes, and write the paper in chunks. In addition, it is also easier for them to organize their information in this manner. The conference is particularly helpful since students know exactly what they need to do to write their final papers. Students now have all the tools they need to write an effective research paper. See Figures 5.10, 5.11, 5.12, and 5.13 for examples of grading criteria (rubrics).

Grading Criteria: Research Process – Proof of the Problem

Criteria	0	1	2	3	4	Score
• Gives background information (answers who, what, when, where, and why) • Examples are clear and specific	Missing	Does not give background information with specific examples	Describes some background information, but several examples lack detail	Describes background information; 1 or 2 examples lack detail	Describes background information with specific examples	____ × 3 = _____
• Examples include use of at least 3 sources that explain and identify the complexity of the problem	Missing	Insufficient sources; does not explain and identify complexity of the problem	Insufficient sources and/or does not explain and/or identify complexity of the problem	Sufficient sources but may not explain or identify the complexity of the problem	Sufficient sources; specifically explains and identifies the complexity of the problem	____ × 2 = _____

_____/20

Figure 5.10

Grading Criteria: Research Process – People/Groups Harmed

Criteria	0	1	2	3	4	Score
• Identifies 3 different groups • Specifically describes harms and effects	Missing	Does not identify 3 different groups or specifically describe harms and effects	Identifies 3 different groups but does not specifically describe harms and effects	Identifies 3 different groups specifically and describes harms and effects, but some parts are unclear	Identifies 3 different groups specifically and describes harms and effects	____ × 3 = _____
• Examples include use of at least 3 sources that explain and identify the complexity of the problem	Missing	Insufficient sources; does not explain the complexity of how the group is harmed	Insufficient sources and/or does not explain the complexity of how the group is harmed	Sufficient sources but may not clearly explain the complexity of how the group is harmed	Sufficient sources; specifically explains the complexity of how the group is harmed	____ × 2 = _____

_____/20

Figure 5.11

Grading Criteria: Research Process – Possible Solutions						
Criteria	**0**	**1**	**2**	**3**	**4**	**Score**
• Identifies 3 solutions • Includes specific examples for each • Explains advantages and disadvantages for each solution	Missing	Identifies 1 solution and gives example; explains advantage and disadvantage for solution	Identifies 2 solutions and gives specific examples for each; explains advantages and disadvantages for each solution	Identifies 3 solutions; gives specific examples for some; explains advantages and disadvantages for some solutions	Identifies 3 solutions and gives specific examples for each; explains advantages and disadvantages for each solution	_____ × 3 = _____
• Examples include use of at least 3 sources for each solution that identifies the complexity of each solution	Missing	Insufficient sources; does not explain the complexity of the solutions	Insufficient sources and/or does not explain the complexity of the solutions	Sufficient sources but may not explain the complexity of the solutions	Sufficient sources; specifically explains the complexity of the solutions	_____ × 2 = _____
						_____ /20

Figure 5.12

CHAPTER SUMMARY

Chapter 5 describes the importance of using a process approach to teach students how to research a topic. In addition, both traditional and nontraditional methods of research are described.

English IV

Name _____

Grading Criteria: Final Research Paper

Not accepted without all parts of the research process, notes, or citations.

Criteria	0	1	2	3	4	Score
Title Page: • strong title • follows format without errors	Missing	Weak title, more than 2 format errors	Good title, 2 format errors	Good title; 1 format error	Strong title; correct format	_____ × 2 =_____
Introduction: • hooks reader • 4–5 sentences	Missing	Poor lead; 1–2 sentences	Weak lead; 2–3 sentences	Good lead; 3–4 sentences	Strong lead; 4–5 sentences	_____ × 3 =_____
Thesis: • defines problem • previews groups and solutions	Missing	Thesis is not complete or clear	Thesis may not be complete and/or clear	Thesis is complete but it lacks clarity	Thesis is complete and specific	_____ × 3 =_____
Proof of the problem: • describes background information (answers who, what, when, where) • explains complexity of problem • minimum 3 citations	Missing	Does not identify background information (answers who, what, when, where) or explain complexity of problem or cite 3 sources	May not identify background information (answers who, what, when, where) and/or explain complexity of problem and/or cite 3 sources	Describes background information (answers who, what, when, where), but may not explain complexity of problem; cites 3 sources	Specifically describes background information (answers who, what, when, where); explains complexity of problem; cites 3 sources	_____ × 5 =_____
Groups Harmed: • identifies 3 groups • explains harm and effect of harm • minimum 2 citations for each group	Missing	Does not identify groups or explain harm and effects of harm; cites 2 sources each	May not identify groups and/or explain harm and effect of harm and/or cite 2 sources each	Identifies groups and explains harm; may not explain effects or give clear example; cites 2 sources each	Specifically identifies groups and explains harm and effect of harm; cites 2 sources each	Group 1 _____ × 5 =_____ Group 2 _____ × 5 =_____ Group 3 _____ × 5 =_____ Total = _____
Solutions: • identifies and explains 3 specific solutions • explains advantages and disadvantages for each • minimum 3 citations each	Missing	Does not clearly identify and explain 3 specific solutions or explain advantages and disadvantages for each; cites 3 sources each	Does not identify and/or explain 3 specific solutions and/or explain advantages and disadvantages for each; cites 3 sources each	Identifies and explains 3 specific solutions, but may not explain advantages and disadvantages for each or clearly cite 3 sources each	Specifically identifies and explains 3 specific solutions and explains advantages and disadvantages for each; cites 3 sources each	Solution 1 _____ × 7 =_____ Solution 2 _____ × 7 =_____ Solution 3 _____ × 7 =_____ Total = _____

Figure 5.13 (continues on next page)

Criteria	0	1	2	3	4	Score
Conclusion: • restates thesis • reviews groups and solutions • call to action	Missing	Does not restate thesis or review groups and solutions or call to action	Does not restate thesis and/or review groups or solutions and/or call to action	Restates thesis; reviews groups and solutions but may not include call to action or lacks clarity	Restates thesis; reviews groups and solutions and call to action	___ × 3 = ___
Style: • clarity of ideas • variety of sentences in length and style • strong vocabulary	Most ideas are not clear; sentences lack variety in length and style; weak vocabulary	Many ideas are not clear; sentences lack variety in length and style; may lack strong vocabulary	Some ideas are not clear; some sentences lack variety in length and/or strong vocabulary	Most ideas are clear; most sentences have variety of length and style; good vocabulary	All ideas are clear; sentences have variety in length and style; strong vocabulary	___ × 2 = ___
Organization: • logical order of ideas throughout • clear transitions	Lack of order and transitions throughout	Lack of order and transitions in several parts	Lacks order or transitions in some parts	Logical order of ideas but weak transitions in some parts	Logical order of ideas and clear transitions throughout	___ × 2 = ___
Grammar: • correct spelling, sentence structure, punctuation, etc.	10 or more errors	9 errors	7–8 errors	5–6 errors	0–4 errors	___ × 6 = ___
Fluency: • minimum of 8 pages typed	4 pages or less	5 pages	6 pages	7 pages	8 or more pages	___ × 1 = ___
Citations: • cites sources in all parts of paper • uses several sources • correct format	Missing	Does not cite sources in all parts of paper; uses few sources; several format errors	Does not cite sources in all parts of paper and/or use several sources; some format errors	Cites sources in all parts of paper; uses several sources; few format errors	Cites sources in all parts of paper and uses several sources; correct format	___ × 5 = ___
Work Cited Page: • cites all sources in paper • does not cite others • correct format	Missing	Does not cite all sources in paper; cites others; several format errors	Does not cite all sources in paper and does not cite others; some format errors	Cites all sources in paper and does not cite others; few format errors	Cites all sources in paper; does not cite others; correct format	___ × 7 = ___

_____/300

Figure 5.13 *(continued)*

COMPUTER CONNECTIONS

1. Have students form triad groups. Then, individually, have each member brainstorm a list of three to five possible research topics. Students then swap the list of topics with another member in the triad. The final task is for the student groups to locate as many Web sites relevant to the research topics as they can in a single class period.

2. Once all triads have completed their Web site searches, they swap their lists with another triad. Their task is to access the Web sites and assess each as to its value, timeliness, reliability, accuracy, validity, and ease of use.

3. Ann Kimpton and Marilyn Payton, Reading Specialists at Willowbrook High School, Villa Park, Illinois, have adapted the I-Search Project in an interesting way. They ask students to create a brochure about a controversial topic outlining the causes and effects of the issue using the computer. The requirements for this project are noted here (Figure 5.14) as well as the I-Search Project Planning Sheet (Figure 5.15).

Criteria for I-Search Paper

A	B/C	F/Incomplete
Organization 1. Analyzes and describes the problem or issue clearly and completely (at least 10 statistics and/or facts). 2. Describes chronology/background of the problem/issue clearly and completely. 3. Analyzes and describes the causes of the problem clearly and completely. 4. Clearly explains the effects of the problem/issue. 5. Explains and supports solutions or opinions to problem/issue clearly and completely. 6. Pamphlet handed in on time (day and period).	1. Analyzes and describes the problem or issue clearly (at least seven statistics and/or facts). 2. Describes chronology/background of the problem/issue. 3. Analyzes and describes the causes of the problem. 4. Explains the effects of the problem/issue. 5. Explains and supports solutions or opinions to problem/issue. 6. Pamphlet handed in up to five days late (specified number of points deducted per day).	1. Does not analyze or describe the problem or issue (six statistics and/or facts or less). 2. Does not describe chronology/background of the problem/issue. 3. Does not analyze and describe the cause of the problem. 4. Does not explain the effects of the problem/issue. 5. Does not explain and support solutions or issues. 6. Pamphlet handed in very late (specified number of points deducted per day).
Thorough Research 1. Information complete and from a variety of sources (more than four sources). 2. Reason/examples given to support opinions and to explain information stated. 3. Information and statistics are accurate.	1. Information complete and from a variety of sources (four sources). 2. Reason/examples given to support opinions and to explain information stated. 3. Information and statistics usually accurate.	1. Information not complete and from a variety of sources (less than four). 2. Reason/examples usually not given to support opinions and to explain information stated. 3. Information and statistics usually inaccurate.
Reflective Thought 1. Writer shows a thorough understanding of the topic. 2. Writer expresses his or her opinion of the topic in a clear, convincing manner.	1. Writer shows a general understanding of the topic. 2. Writer expresses his or her opinion of the topic.	1. Writer does not show an understanding of the topic. 2. Writer expresses his or her opinion of the topic.
Involvement of the Reader 1. The opinion of the writer is easy to understand. 2. The pamphlet attracts the attention of the reader. 3. Questions or statements encourage the reader to think about the topic.	1. The opinion of the writer is understandable. 2. The reader is interested in the pamphlet. 3. Questions or statements are considered by the reader.	1. The opinion of the writer is not understandable. 2. The pamphlet is not interesting to the reader. 3. The reader is not encouraged to consider the topic.

Figure 5.14 *(continues on next page)*

Criteria for I-Search Paper

A	B/C	F/Incomplete
Appearance and Mechanics 1. The pamphlet is creative and attractive. 2. Pamphlet is free of spellng or punctuation errors. 3. Professional appearance (no pencil). 4. Use of more than one graphic. 5. Note cards handed in with pamphlet.	1. The pamphlet is neat and clear. 2. The pamphlet has a minimal number of spelling or punctuation errors (three or four). 3. Professional appearance (no pencil). 4. Use of at least one graphic. 5. Note cards handed in with pamphlet.	1. The pamphlet is carelessly done. 2. The pamphlet has a large number of spelling or punctuation errors. 3. Done in pencil. 4. No graphics. 5. No note cards.
Bibliography 1. More than four sources are listed. 2. Sources are listed according to the format shown in the directions in all cases. 3. Bibliography cards handed in with pamphlet.	1. At least four sources are used. 2. Sources are generally listed according to the format shown in the directions. 3. Bibliography cards handed in with pamphlet.	1. Less than four sources are used. 2. Sources are not listed according to the format shown in the directions. 3. Bibliography cards not handed in.

Developed by Ann Kimpton and Marilyn Payton, Willowbrook High School, Villa Park, Illinois.

Figure 5.14 *(continued)*

I-Search Project Planning Sheet

Directions: Complete the following in preparation for the Controversial I-Search Brochure Proposal.

1. What subject do you wish to study for your research project?

2. What are the two sides of the issue?

3. At this point, what side of the issue do you tend to support?

4. Write a few sentences explaining why you want to study this topic and why you believe it is a worthwhile topic to study.

5. Do you know any individual or organization you could contact to help you gather information on your topic? If so, list them below.

Developed by Ann Kimpton and Marilyn Payton, Willowbrook High School, Villa Park, Illinois.

Figure 5.15

Teacher Tips

❶ After students have completed the activities listed here, create a file of useful Web sites for future use.

❷ Use the following Blackline Masters to make the research process more manageable:

   a. Newspaper Research Project: Student Guidelines Checklist (Figure 5.16)

   b. Menu of Activities for Newspaper Research Project (Figure 5.17)

   c. Traditional Research Process Approach (Figure 5.18)

   d. Traditional Research Process Checklist (Figure 5.19)

Newspaper Research Project: Student Guidelines Checklist

Directions: Follow these steps to create a newspaper that focuses on a specific time period in a person's life.

1. Choose an older person to interview, preferably a family member: a great grandparent, grandparent, or an older aunt or uncle. If you do not have an older extended relative, choose an older friend of the family.

2. Remember to focus on a specific time period in the person's life (for example, the years 1930–35).

3. Look at the menu of activities to see which ones interest you and your person. Prepare a list of questions that will help you fulfill the requirements for the activities you choose.

   a. Remember that everyone needs to complete #1 (people profile) and #9 (personal profile).

   b. In addition, choose three 16-point activities from #2, #3, #4, #6, and #8 and one 20-point activity from #5 or #7.

4. Keep the notes from your interview as they are considered primary sources.

5. Take notes on index cards and keep track of the bibliographical information as you read the secondary sources needed to complete this project.

6. Use all of your notes as you create the newspaper.

7. Follow the grading criteria for both parts of this research project.

8. Follow the calendar to meet all due dates.

Figure 5.16

Menu of Activities for Newspaper Research Project

Directions: Have students circle their choices.
Guidelines:
1. Everyone must complete #1 (people profile) and #9 (personal profile) from the menu.
2. Choose **one** 20-point activity: #5 (editorial) or #7 (home life).
3. Choose **three** 16-point activities; #2 (travel), #3 (obituary), #4 (entertainment), #6 (advice column), and #8 (classified).

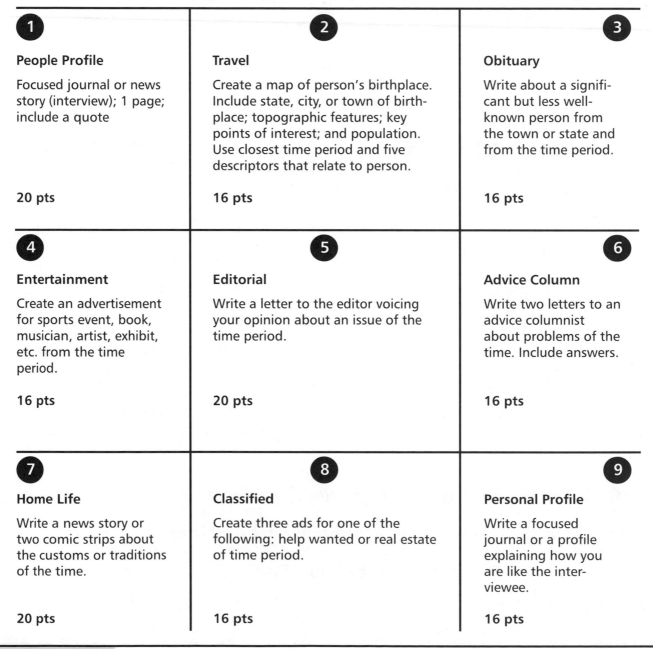

1

People Profile

Focused journal or news story (interview); 1 page; include a quote

20 pts

2

Travel

Create a map of person's birthplace. Include state, city, or town of birthplace; topographic features; key points of interest; and population. Use closest time period and five descriptors that relate to person.

16 pts

3

Obituary

Write about a significant but less well-known person from the town or state and from the time period.

16 pts

4

Entertainment

Create an advertisement for sports event, book, musician, artist, exhibit, etc. from the time period.

16 pts

5

Editorial

Write a letter to the editor voicing your opinion about an issue of the time period.

20 pts

6

Advice Column

Write two letters to an advice columnist about problems of the time. Include answers.

16 pts

7

Home Life

Write a news story or two comic strips about the customs or traditions of the time.

20 pts

8

Classified

Create three ads for one of the following: help wanted or real estate of time period.

16 pts

9

Personal Profile

Write a focused journal or a profile explaining how you are like the interviewee.

16 pts

Figure 5.17

Traditional Research Process Approach

The student and/or the teacher can use this form as an individual checklist.
Key = 0 incomplete, * = partially complete, or + = completed satisfactorily.

Student's Name _____	Assessment Key
1. Newspaper article	
2. Journal activity	
3. 10 questions about topic	
4. Analyzing topic	
5. Completed 3 bibliography cards and 3 note cards	
6. Thesis	
7. Proof of the problem	
8. Groups hurt	
9. Solution	
10. Preliminary outline	

Figure 5.18

Traditional Research Process Checklist

Teachers can use this form as a checklist for the whole class.

Key: 0 = incomplete   * = partially complete or needs work   + = completed satisfactorily

Student's Name	Newspaper article	Journal activity	10 questions about topic	Analyzing topic activities	Completed three bibliography cards and three source cards	Thesis	Proof of the problem	Groups hurt	Solution	Preliminary outline

Figure 5.19

Integrating Reading and Writing in the Classroom

We do not write in order to be understood; we write in order to understand. . . .

C. Day Lewis

THE READING-WRITING CONNECTION

CHARACTERISTICS OF EFFECTIVE READING AND WRITING STRATEGIES

FOSTERING CRITICAL UNDERSTANDING

ENGAGING READERS AND WRITERS IN THE PROCESS OF REVISION
- Generating Interactions Between Schema and Text (GIST)
- The Reader's Questions*
- Fact Acrostic

FOSTERING PRIOR KNOWLEDGE
- KWL Plus*
- KND Chart*

ENCOURAGING STUDENTS TO BECOME PERSONALLY INVOLVED
- Reading from Different Perspectives*
- Discussion Web*
- RAFT

ASKING STUDENTS TO INVOKE PERSONAL FEELINGS
- Possible Dialogues
- Journals and Learning Logs
  - Double-Entry Journal
- Biography Poem*

CHAPTER SUMMARY

*Indicates that a Blackline Master is included in Teacher Tips at the end of the chapter.

THE READING-WRITING CONNECTION

Whereas reading and writing were once considered separate skills, today we recognize the important relationship between them. In our classrooms, we often see that students who are avid readers are usually good writers as well. It naturally follows that as they read more, they tend to write more. These good readers-writers also tend to have a positive image of their literacy abilities and, as a result, are anxious to utilize their skills to read and write on their own a great deal. In effect, then, reading and writing have a symbiotic relationship—that is, when used together, they are greater than the sum of their parts, and their combination helps to foster critical learning (Shanahan 1990).

Reading and writing are both constructive processes, and during these processes, information is organized in some fashion and then accommodated as part of our memory structures (Squire 1983). Current research also clarifies how both the writer and the reader are involved in the construction of meaning because the writer tries to create a clear text, while the reader tries to understand that text (Vacca and Vacca 1996). The active interchange that takes place between the reader, writer, and text creates a sort of "text world." Building this text world results in learning (Konopak, Martin, and Martin 1987). In addition, when students are asked to read text and then write a response to it, they must construct their own representations of what they have learned. Then, through thinking processes such as synthesis, evaluation, and summarization, they refine that representation to make images of their own (McKenna and Robinson 1990). Furthermore, when students read and then write in their content areas, they acquire the basic vocabulary of that discipline; they learn the technical terms of the discipline in context as well as how language is used in that specific content area. In essence, students learn to read, write, and think like scientists, mathematicians, artists, historians, and the like (Squire 1983). As a result, their achievement improves (Shanahan 1990).

CHARACTERISTICS OF EFFECTIVE READING AND WRITING STRATEGIES

Reading and writing are important tools for learning from text. A myriad of strategies that combine these two processes exists. In an effort to identify strategies that best support student learning, we first searched to identify the characteristics of effective reading-writing strategies, then located strategies containing these characteristics, and finally provided detailed explanations and examples of those strategies.

After an extensive examination of many reading-writing strategies, McGee and Richgels (1990) concluded that effective reading-writing strategies contain five major characteristics. They should (1) foster critical understanding; (2) engage readers and writers in the process of revision; (3) provide steps during which students carefully and thoroughly assess, monitor, and use their prior knowledge of topics being studied; (4) encourage students to become personally involved in the texts they are reading and writing by providing activities that ask them to make choices, take positions, or view topics from a different perspective; and (5) ask students to carefully examine, assess, utilize, and possibly monitor their personal feelings about the topics they are reading. In essence, strategies that contain these characteristics work to foster both the cognitive and affective domains. In the following sections, we will discuss each of these five characteristics in detail and then provide strategies that use them.

FOSTERING CRITICAL UNDERSTANDING

There are many definitions of critical thinking or understanding. We have heard it defined as problem solving, higher-order thinking, divergent thinking, and analytical thinking. Thus, it seems safe to assert that critical understanding requires students to be active thinkers who thoughtfully and carefully reflect upon the concepts and ideas they are reading and then form their own ideas about those concepts. In essence, it involves more than merely asking students to memorize names, places, and events. Instead, students must evaluate what they have read, deliberate upon it, weigh the evidence presented, follow logical reasoning processes, come to conclusions, pose new or alternative questions, consider other possibilities, and apply what they have learned to new situations. If students reading about AIDS consider its ramifications on our culture twenty years from now, they will have a far deeper understanding than if they just recited its causes, complications, and preventions. Similarly, when students investigating hurricanes predict the impact of today's level-five hurricane on the economy or environment for the next ten years rather than merely citing what conditions give rise to the creation of a hurricane, they are exercising critical thinking skills.

ENGAGING READERS AND WRITERS IN THE PROCESS OF REVISION

As good teachers, we recognize the value of the revision step in the writing process. However, we sometimes tend to overlook this step when thinking about the reading process. Yet, Fitzgerald (1989) points out that revision is probably crucial to the development of students' critical thinking processes. In addition, McGee and Richgels (1990) pose that during the revision process in reading, students must take time to reflect and revisit the text, thinking about it from different perspectives. Realizing this, we are able to easily spot the revision process in reading at work. We revise whenever we choose to reread a favorite book and suddenly see a new facet of it we had not realized before. What adult does not appreciate the message provided by Van Allsburg in *The Polar Express* or by Dr. Seuss in *Oh, The Places You'll Go!*, a message they may have missed during an earlier reading of those wonderful books? Revision in reading takes the reader on an exquisite journey that encourages reflection, rethinking, and the realizations of new perspectives, surely the same wonderful journey taken by writers as they hone their work to perfection. Following are three strategies that foster critical understanding and engage readers and writers in revision.

Generating Interactions Between Schema and Text (GIST)

Based on Cunningham's (1982) "Generating Interactions between Schemata and Text," GIST is a strategy that works to improve students' reading comprehension and summary writing skills by honing their abilities to analyze and synthesize content area readings. This strategy offers many advantages to students who use it. Students must use synthesis and analysis in order to effectively summarize the text read. By restricting the length of the passage, students learn to delete trivial information, determine main ideas, and use their own words to make generalizations—three major strategies that have been recognized as crucial for good comprehension and retention of key ideas (Kintch and Van Dijk 1978). So that students can watch the processes of active thinking and reflecting in action, the teacher should model this strategy before students use it independently. This strategy also fosters the verbal/linguistic and interpersonal intelligences.

 Steps for GIST

1. From your content area text, choose a three to five paragraph passage that discusses an important concept. Reproduce it on an overhead transparency.

2. Show the students the first paragraph of the passage. Have them read it silently and then write a twenty words or less summary of the passage. Encourage them to use as many of their own words as possible in their writing.

3. Using the individual summaries students wrote as a basis for discussion, generate a class summary.

4. Show the next paragraph and again have students write a summary of twenty words or less encompassing paragraphs one and two.

5. Continue this process until a GIST statement has been developed for the entire passage. Encourage students to use no more than forty to fifty words in their final summaries.

6. After practice, students will be able to generate GIST statements on their own.

This strategy can be used in any content area. It can be used in language arts with novels, short stories, and poems. In addition, it can be used with chapter sections that contain difficult concepts in social studies, mathematics, science, or health. See Figure 6.1 for an example of its use.

A GIST Statement for Science

Developed during the reading of a section on stem growth.

After reading of first paragraph:
Plant cells able to divide are found in two places in stems—between vascular tissues in vascular bundles and in buds. **(21 words)**

After reading of second paragraph:
Plant cells able to divide are found between tissues in vascular bundles of stems, which cause them to widen, and in buds. Herbaceous but not woody, they die yearly. **(29 words)**

After reading of third paragraph:
Plant cells able to divide are found between tissues in vascular bundles of stems and in buds. Each year herbaceous stems die, but woody ones produce a new layer. The old layer becomes bark. **(34 words)**

After reading of fourth paragraph:
Plant cells that divide to widen stems are found between tissues in vascular bundles and those that lengthen stems in the buds. Each year herbaceous stems die, but woody stems produce a new layer. Cell growth in buds lengthens stems and makes leaves. **(43 words)**

Figure 6.1

I like it when our teacher uses one concept to unify all of our classes, but I'm really sick of the theme. How about you?

The Reader's Questions

Students often have a difficult time or little interest in reading textbooks. The reader's questions—*who, what, when, where, why,* and *how*—provide an anticipatory set or framework for reading. As students read, they record their responses in a graphic organizer, or chart, that will help them to identify main points from the content. Since students may need to reread parts of the text to complete the chart, this strategy aids in comprehension, organizing information, stimulating thinking, and helping students connect to the content. The graphic organizer also serves as a memory tool and can be used in class discussions. By using this strategy, students enrich their verbal/linguistic, logical/ mathematical, visual/spatial, intrapersonal, and interpersonal intelligences.

 Steps for Using Reader's Questions

See Teacher Tips at the end of this chapter for a Blackline Master to use with this strategy (Figure 6.13).

1. Provide students with some direction for using these questions as they can take a number of different directions. Here are some sample questions:
   a. Who (is the person and who were other key people in his or her life)?
   b. When and where (did the person live, travel, or become successful)?
   c. What were the person's beliefs?
   d. What (were his or her problems, adventures, failures, ideas)?
   e. How (did he or she solve problems, relate with others, achieve recognition)?
   f. Why was the person important?
2. Prepare a chart that will guide students while (or after) they read.
3. Use the same question framework after they discuss the text, and then ask, "What if . . . happened?"

Figure 6.2 provides a sample of Reader's Questions for the language arts classroom. This strategy can be used in any content area. It can be used in mathematics with measurements and word problems; in social studies to study the Civil War; in science to examine hurricanes or dinosaurs; and in art to consider the great artists.

Sample Reader's Questions for Language Arts				
WHO: Henry David Thoreau of Walden Pond				
WHEN AND WHERE (time and place)	WHAT (beliefs)	WHAT (problems)	HOW (solutions)	WHY (were ideas important)
1840 Massachusetts	Materialism promotes the wrong values.	He wouldn't teach at the public school since flogging was used to discipline.	He set up his own school but ran out of money.	He kept a journal of his actions/ideas.
1845 Massachusetts	He turned to nature to nourish spirit and mind.	He owed $1.50 for poll tax.	He refused to pay tax because it aided war. He went to jail.	Transcendental philosophy Civil disobedience

Figure 6.2

Fact Acrostic

Teachers frequently use *acrostics,* a type of word game, to have students create a simple poetic form, "name" poetry. Students write their names down the page, one letter per line, and write descriptions of themselves for each letter. The letters of their names serve as a mnemonic device to help them produce a descriptor that fits each letter. The Fact Acrostic is a variation of this popular poetry form that asks students to use topics found in the content area for the term(s) and to create the "poem" by describing facts and ideas that are related (Johnston 1985). Since students may need to reread the text to complete the acrostic, they will enhance their own knowledge about the topic and use their creative abilities to transfer the information into a poetic form. Students also develop their verbal/linguistic, logical/mathematical, interpersonal, and intrapersonal intelligences.

Steps for a Fact Acrostic

1. Instruct students to write the letters of the content area topic down the page.
2. Have students write a fact about the topic in each line of the poem.
3. Encourage students to produce a poem based on the topic.

Figure 6.3 provides a Fact Acrostic for mathematics. This strategy can be used in any content area. It can be used in social studies to investigate cultures, mythology, and ways of life; in science to examine animal life or the solar system; and in the fine arts to explore styles of painting and schools of music.

A Mathematics Acrostic

E qual signs are used

Q uantities are measured

U ses complex variables

A Formula

T wo fundamental characteristics: identities and conditions

I n a linear area

O perations are separated on the left sides and right sides

N umbers are denoted by symbols

Figure 6.3

FOSTERING PRIOR KNOWLEDGE

A plethora of reading research substantiates the fact that the more students know about a subject they will study, the better they will comprehend what they are asked to read. Spilich, Vesonder, Chiesi, and Voss (1979) illustrated this idea well in their research using subjects who differed in their knowledge of baseball but did not differ in their level of reading comprehension. Students who had a high level of prior knowledge about baseball were able to comprehend and recall information they read about a fictitious game, because they were able to rely on their background knowledge to draw correct inferences when faced with implicit rather than explicit facts.

Roberta Sejnost witnessed firsthand the effect of prior knowledge on comprehension when she was completing an internship at an inner-city college reading clinic. One day, in an effort to reach a reluctant middle school student, she proposed that the student read a catchy story about a family fishing trip. He read, and Roberta asked him questions about what he had been reading. All went well until he came to a section of the story that discussed how a grandfather had spent the afternoon teaching his young grandson how to tie flies. Strangely enough, her student's comprehension of the story fell flat. After much discussion, he posed this question to Roberta: "Just tell me this: how did that grandfather manage to tie those feathers on the fly without crushing him?" Suddenly, the comprehension problem became crystal clear: this young man had never been fishing, much less ever used a fishing fly. His only experience with flies was with those that buzzed around in the air. What a perfect example of the power of prior knowledge! Following are two strategies that foster prior knowledge: KWL Plus and KND chart.

KWL Plus

See Teacher Tips at the end of this chapter for a Blackline Master to use with this strategy (Figure 6.14).

All teachers of literacy know that, to be successful, active readers make use of a process as they read. They foster prior knowledge; they establish a purpose or know what they are looking for as they read; they are attentive to what they are reading; they evaluate what they read; they often seek additional information from outside sources; and they are able to summarize the main ideas of what they have learned, often by using a graphic organizer. The strategy, KWL Plus (Carr and Ogle 1987), provides practice in all of these crucial steps of the reading to learn process. The K stands for *know*, the W for *want* to know, and the L for have *learned*. The Plus refers to the summary which students write using the concept map they have created.

Before reading, students' prior knowledge about a topic is activated and fostered through questioning and discussion. As the strategy plays out, the teacher guides students through a process that models active thinking and questioning skills and encourages them to set a purpose or focus for their reading. Students complete a four-column graphic organizer. This organizer, which keeps students engaged and attentive to their reading, can easily be used as a guide as students read the assigned text. Finally, students are encouraged to seek outside sources for answers to questions that were not answered in the assigned text and then write a summary of information learned as the final step in this process. This strategy also has the potential to foster the verbal/linguistic, logical/mathematical, visual/spatial, intrapersonal, and interpersonal intelligences.

Steps for KWL Plus

1. Ask students to recall what they *know* or think they know about a topic. Record this in the K column of the graphic organizer.

2. Encourage students to generate their own questions about the topic as they complete the K portion of the organizer. At this point, help them determine what they *want to know* about the subject and tell them to record this in the W section of the organizer. Include questions generated earlier as well as all additional questions that they pose.

3. Students are now ready to read the text. Tell them to look for answers to the questions they generated for the W section of the organizer as well as for any other information that expands their knowledge and understanding of the topic. Advise them to record what they *have learned* in the L portion of the organizer.

4. After students have read, have them categorize the information they have learned and record it in the graphic organizer section entitled Categories of Information We Expect to Use. Help students weave this information into a concept map that organizes the information and serves as a basis for writing assignments such as summarizing, analyzing, and evaluating.

See Figure 6.4 for a useful way to use the KWL Plus Grid in your science classroom and Figure 6.5 for an alternative example of a KWL Plus Concept Map.

KND Chart

See Teacher Tips at the end of this chapter for a Blackline Master to use with this strategy (Figure 6.15).

A variation of the KWL Plus, the KND, can be used for research or for problem-based learning (Fogarty 1997). Students use the chart to list facts that they *know* about the topic (K), thus, activating their prior knowledge. Next, they generate questions about what they *need* to know about the topic (N). These questions check for their understanding and ask them to search for in-depth knowledge about the content as well as connections to life. Then students make a list of things they need to *do* (D) to answer their questions. The list helps them prioritize their needs, identify specific areas for research, and set goals. Since students use a graphic organizer to record their information, they can easily visualize their ideas and get practice in summarizing, categorizing, and prioritizing their needs. The KND chart fosters verbal/linguistic, logical/mathematical, visual/spatial, intrapersonal, and interpersonal intelligences. Refer to Figure 6.6 to see how it can be used in the science classroom.

KWL Plus Grid for Science		
Types of Rocks		
K (Know)	**W (Want to Know)**	**L (Have Learned)**
1. There are three kinds of rocks.	1. What are the names of the three kinds of rocks?	1. Sedimentary rocks form in sedimentary layers. (S)
2. The hardest rock is the diamond.	2. How fast does it take to form a rock?	2. It takes millions of years to make rocks. (C)
3. Rocks form underground.	3. What is a rock cycle?	3. Sedimentary can change to metamorphic. (S)
4. Rocks come in a variety of colors.	4. How is a rock formed?	4. Igneous rocks are formed by heat. (I)
5. Rocks can be found on land and in water.	5. Can rocks be formed from other rocks?	5. Metamorphic rocks were once sedimentary. (M)
6. Lava turns into rock.	6. How old are rocks?	6. Metamorphic rocks were once igneous. (M)
	7. Are rocks found on other planets?	7. Igneous rocks are formed by lava. (I)
	8. How do rocks get their colors?	8. Rocks go through cycles. (C)
	9. What type of rock is the heaviest?	9. Rocks keep changing. (C)
	10. What type of rock is the lightest?	10. A rock cycle is something that repeats itself. (C)
		11. Heat, pressure, and weathering cause rocks to change. (C)
		12. Rocks can change from one type to another type. (C)
		13. Igneous rocks can change to metamorphic. (I)
Categories of Information We Expect To Use		
C = Changes in rocks **I** = Igneous **S** = Sedimentary **M** = Metamorphic		
Developed by Maribeth Ewald, St. Xavier University's Field-Based Master's Program, Hanover Park, Illinois.		

Figure 6.4

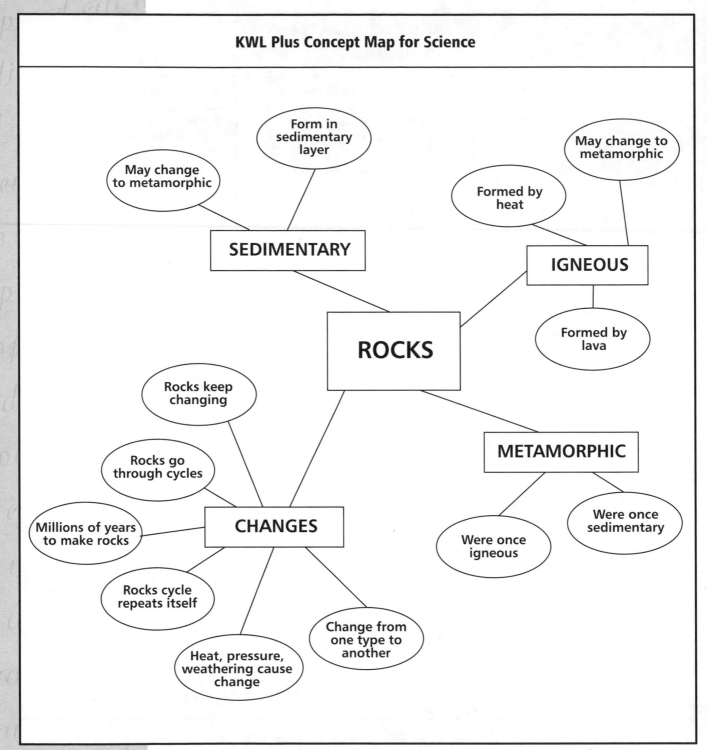

Figure 6.5

KND Chart for Science		
Types of Rocks		
What Do We Know? (K)	**What Do We Want to Know?** (N)	**What Do We Need to Do?** (D)
1. There are three kinds of rocks.	1. Which types of rocks exist?	1. Read class text(s).
2. The hardest rock is the diamond.	2. What are the characteristics of each type?	2. Do library research.
3. Rocks form underground.	3. How do rocks change?	3. Do Internet research.
4. Rocks come in a variety of colors.		4. Visit the Natural History Museum.
5. Rocks can be found on land and in water.		5. Interview a geologist.
6. Lava turns into rock.		6. Interview a rock collector.
		7. Look for educational videos on rocks.

Figure 6.6

This strategy can be used in any content area. In language arts, it can be used to study topics from novels, short stories, and grammar as well as in prewriting activities. In social studies, it can be utilized to investigate historical eras, great leaders, wars, countries, and states. Mathematics teachers may use it to help students learn about polygons, angles, general mathematic facts, and great mathematicians. Science teachers can use it to teach about volcanoes, dinosaurs, rocks, chemicals, and photosynthesis. Finally, in the fine arts classroom, teachers can use the strategy to facilitate learning about composers and artists as well as about different types of art and music.

ENCOURAGING STUDENTS TO BECOME PERSONALLY INVOLVED

We are all aware that we perform better when we are personally involved in a task. Roberta Sejnost often jokes with her family that if they had company once a week she would have an immaculate house because her company cleaning is much different from her regular cleaning. Students react in much the same way. McGee and Richgels (1990) suggest that students become personally involved in their reading and writing when asked to defend a position. Thus, students must first read the text and then reflect not only on its meaning, but also on how that meaning might differ when looked at from a different perspective. Imagine the different responses students might give if they recited the facts of the Civil War from any one of these perspectives: a southern general; a northern general; the mother of a slain soldier; a northern youth whose brother fought and died for the south; a slave in the south; a freedman in the north; a plantation owner; President Lincoln; or a doctor. Following are several strategies to encourage students to become personally involved.

Reading from Different Perspectives

A strategy that asks students to become personally involved is Reading from Different Perspectives (McNeil 1984). As individuals, we all have opinions and biases toward subjects. Furthermore, many times these opinions and biases affect how we come to understand and relate to the subject. As parents, we view the issue of a fair curfew much differently than our children do; as teachers, we may consider pagers in our classrooms a disturbance, yet some of our students consider them a necessity.

The strategy of Reading from Different Perspectives encourages students to engage in repeated readings of a text in order to gain a fuller, more complete understanding of it as well as to appreciate the topic from a perspective other than their own. First, students read the selection from a specific perspective, one either self-chosen or designated by the teacher. As the students read from this perspective, they seek to identify what needs and concerns someone with that perspective might have. Next, students reread and reflect on what they have read, going into the text to seek out specific details about items they noted as needs or concerns; they should also make a personal reaction to those text statements. As a final step, students come to grips with the issue being studied by creating a position statement summarizing their feelings about the issue from the perspective they have assumed.

As students move through this process, their verbal/linguistic, visual/spatial, logical/mathematical, interpersonal, and intrapersonal intelligences are developed. In addition, they become active readers as they read and reread the text, monitoring and evaluating their understanding as they search for specific details to support their reflections. For best results, the teacher should model this strategy before students use it independently.

 ## *Steps for Reading from Different Perspectives*

See Teacher Tips at the end of this chapter for a Blackline Master to use with this strategy (Figure 6.16).

1. Ask students to read the selection and identify several perspectives from which the selection can be viewed. Until students are practiced in using this strategy, the teacher may want to identify the perspectives for them or guide them in determining the perspectives.

2. Then assign a different perspective to each student or each group.

3. Have students reread the selection to determine possible needs and concerns of someone holding their assigned perspective.

4. Once students identify these needs and concerns, have students reread the selection to locate specific details that substantiate the noted needs and concerns. Invite students to personally react to those details.

5. As a final step, tell students to write a summary of their perspective in a position statement.

This strategy can be used in any content area. For social studies, students can examine the concept of immigration from the perspective of an immigration officer, the parent whose children have been left in another country, a resident, or even a US laborer who fears his or her job might be threatened by immigrant workers. In science, students can consider the effects of pesticides from the perspective of a plant, a gardener, a bug, or the meat industry. Figure 6.7 gives an example of Reading from Different Perspectives for a social studies lesson.

Reading from Different Perspectives for Social Studies

ARTICLE/TEXT/TOPIC: Whales Trapped in Ice
FROM THE PERSPECTIVE OF: Trapped, dying whale

NEEDS	CONCERNS
Open sea	Frozen water
To breed	Not enough food
Warm water	Space
Someone to understand my problem	No way to communicate

SUPPORT and PERSONAL REACTIONS

Text Support Statements	My Reactions
I waited too long, and now I am surrounded by ice.	Help me! I have no space to swim or to breathe!
They are using chainsaws to cut through the ice; they are making me breathing holes.	Thank goodness! A breath of fresh air is coming soon.
Oh, the water is getting too shallow!	Help! I must have deeper water or I will die; I am so afraid.
Wait, what is the old Inuit saying? I can understand him; he is using the ancient signs of his ancestors to talk to me.	I may be saved yet. Perhaps man is not as evil as I began to think he was!

SUMMARY POSITION STATEMENT

The frozen sea was very scary and quite treacherous for me. Luckily, the Americans and the Inuit were able to help me escape. I especially loved being able to communicate with the Inuit Taloom. He was the only one who realized my need and knew the ancient ways to talk to me. Perhaps man and nature can become friends again after all!

Figure 6.7

Discussion Web

The Discussion Web (Alvermann 1991) is a strategy to help students examine an issue from alternative viewpoints, thereby fostering critical thinking while promoting active discussion. Students read an assignment that offers alternative views to a topic, discuss a central question about the topic, identify alternative viewpoints to the question, and weigh the views. Then, in a cooperative group setting, they come to a conclusion, recording all their thought processes on a graphic organizer.

Students first think about the question and identify their own ideas about it. Next, they meet with a partner to share ideas and to generate a list of pro and con responses to the question. This pair joins another pair to share responses and to reach a group consensus on the question. This consensus response, together with one major supporting reason, is presented to the class in the final step of the process. As students move through this process, their verbal/linguistic, visual/spatial, logical/mathematical, interpersonal, and intrapersonal intelligences are developed. As always, the teacher should model this strategy for students.

 Steps for a Discussion Web

See Teacher Tips at the end of this chapter for a Blackline Master to use with this strategy (Figure 6.17).

1. Divide students into pairs; distribute graphic organizer sheet.
2. Assign reading and identify a "controversial" question students will discuss after the reading is completed.
3. Explain that as they read they are to locate and write down reasons/evidence from the reading that supports both a yes and a no response to the question.
4. Have students read the selection silently or out loud and write evidence for each alternative viewpoint. Note: For every reason on the Yes side there should be a reason on the No side. Students write their reasons on the graphic organizer.
5. When the reading is finished, instruct the pairs to join another pair of students to compare or discuss the evidence they have gathered for both sides of the question.
6. Require that the four students reach a consensus on a yes/no conclusion and decide which one reason best supports their conclusion. Remind them that if they do not agree on one conclusion, they must choose a conclusion most of them agree on. (Tip: Allow only one

support reason from each group; this gives students practice in prioritizing and eliminates the possibility that groups who report later in the class period will say that all the reasons have already been presented.)

7. Ask for one student from each group of four to present the group's conclusion and reason. (Tip: Select "presenter" at the last moment; this encourages more engaged participation and listening by all group members as they work.)

8. To bring a personal close to this activity, ask each student to respond to these questions: What conclusion did I *personally* come to? What is the best reason to support this conclusion?

9. As a final step, ask the whole group to reflect on what they learned from using the Discussion Web process. Consider these questions:

   - Did focusing on a question before you read help you understand the reading better?
   - Did searching for evidence as you read help you understand the reading better?
   - What was the most difficult step of the process? Why?
   - Which step do you think best helped you understand? Explain.
   - Did you change your mind about the question during any step of the process? Explain.

This strategy can be used in any content area. There are many possibilities for questions. In social studies, you can ask if men should be paid higher wages than women since they are often considered to be the family breadwinners. In science, you can inquire if aerosol sprays should be eliminated. In technology or business classes, you can discuss if all students should be taught to use Windows 2000 software. In language arts, inquire if Little Willy won the race fairly in the novel *Stone Fox*. Finally, in health, debate whether emergency room doctors should report accident victims they suspect may have been driving while under the influence of alcohol or drugs.

Figure 6.8 shows an example of a Discussion Web that deals with the topic of the death penalty.

Example Discussion Web

Reasons For

1. Such a harsh punishment would decrease crime.

2. They deserve the same punishment as they gave; "an eye for an eye."

3. The death penalty prevents overcrowding in jails.

4. This would save taxpayers money because we would not have to pay for their food and upkeep.

5. Victim's families would feel avenged, and it would bring closure to their grief.

6. This makes sure felons are not parolled to commit heinous crimes again.

REASONS

Yes   The Death Penalty should be upheld   No

CONCLUSION

Reasons Against

1. One evil act should not lead to another. Killing is wrong no matter who does it.

2. What if evidence later shows them to be innocent? if they are dead, it is too late.

3. Sometimes people do things because they are mentally ill and need help. Killing them does not help them.

4. The death penalty punishes the criminal's family because it takes a loved one's life.

5. No one has the right to take another life.

6. People have a right to be rehabilitated.

What was your GROUP'S consensus? My group felt that the Death Penalty should be abolished because it was barbaric.

What was your PERSONAL opinion? I believe that the Death Penalty should be upheld because it will serve to deter other criminals, because if they know they will get the death penalty, they will think twice about killing someone.

What part of the Discussion Web process BEST helped you understand the selection? Having to find reasons both for and against really helped me think about what I was reading and how to make sense of it better!

Figure 6.8

RAFT

RAFT (Santa 1988) is an acronym for *role, audience, format,* and *topic,* the key elements located in every good writing assignment. Specifically, RAFT is best defined in the following way:

R = Role of the writer (Who is the writer? What role does he or she play?)

A = Audience for the writer (To whom are you writing? Who will read your writing?)

F = Format of the writing (What form will your writing take?)

T = Topic of the writing (What will you be writing about?)

This strategy offers many advantages to students who use it. The specificity and focus of the writing assignments make writing more enjoyable for students. As students become personally involved in their topic, they begin to look at an issue from a different perspective. More importantly, they write for a specific audience rather than for the teacher. This step in the process promotes active thinking and reflecting, because students must process the information read rather than merely write answers to questions. Finally, the strategy fosters verbal/linguistic and intrapersonal intelligences. For best results, the teacher should model this strategy before students use it independently.

 Steps for RAFT

1. Guide students as they analyze the important ideas, concepts, or information from the reading assignment. (Topic)
2. With students, brainstorm possible roles class members could assume in their writing. (Role)
3. Next, ask students to decide who the audience will be for this writing. (Audience)
4. Finally, determine the format the writing will take. (Format)
5. For the students' first experience with this strategy, you may want to assign all students the same role for their writing. In subsequent lessons, you should encourage students to brainstorm their own role, audience, and format.

This strategy can be used in any content area; see the possible RAFT assignments (Figure 6.9a) and RAFT example (Figure 6.9b).

ROLE	AUDIENCE	FORMAT	TOPIC
RAFT Assignments			
Macbeth	People of England	Letter of apology	Greed for the throne
Astronaut	NASA	Records of flights	Discoveries
Ben Franklin	Readers	Memoirs	Adventures in Boston
Preacher	Congregation	Sermon	Safety in schools
Principal	Student body	Instructions	School evacuation plan
Mom	Daughter	Recipe	Holiday dessert
Journalist	Readers	News release	Hostage situation
Robert Browning	Readers	Love poem	Feelings about Elizabeth Browning (his wife)
Lawyer	Jury	Appeal	Leniency for death row inmate
Newspaper reporter	Readers during the Great Depression	Obituary	Qualities of teenage hobo
Frontier woman	Self	Diary	Hardships settling in the West
Constituent	US Senator	Letter	Gun control
Journalist	Public	News release	Steps in solving a linear equation
Archeologist	Chemical company	Instructions	Use of diffusion/osmosis in mummification
Cheeseburger	Fat cell	Travel guide	Journey/blood stream
Microscope	Student	Brochure	How to use or care for me
Algebraic equation	Parentheses	Love letter	What parentheses do for equations
Goldfish	First grade students	Plea	Set up a healthy fish tank
Advertiser	Sunscreen manufacturer	Pamphlet	How to prevent skin cancer
Advice columnist	Troubled polynomial couple	Dear Abby reply	Disagreements
Treble clef	Bass clef	Friendly letter	How they are different
Roots	Worm	Dialogue	Function of roots
Water	Seedlings	Poem	How water helps

Figure 6.9a

SkyLight Professional Development

RAFT Assignment for Mathematics

Assignment:

R = Rational number (proper or improper)
A = Another fraction
F = Letter
T = How fractions work together to produce a sum, difference, quotient, or product

Dear 3/4,

I was watching the news the other day, and the reporters showed a segment that caught my attention. It was an activity that I thought would make us better friends. I know we have been drifting apart lately, so I thought this exercise would make us friends again.

Here is my idea. I will stand next to you, and we put out a division sign between us. Then you do a headstand, and we change that sign to multiplication. If we are wearing the same type of pants or sweaters, we can turn them into shorts and t-shirts. Then we multiply ourselves together. We put my t-shirt with your shorts and my shorts with your t-shirt. If it is possible, we can make our shorts and t-shirts a little bit smaller.

I think that this will make us closer than ever. Included in my letter is an example. Let me know what you think.

Love,
6/12

$$6/12 \div 3/4 = ?$$
$$6/12 \cdot 4/3 = 24/36 = 2/3$$
$$2/3 \cdot 1/1 = 2/3 = \text{What we would be if we were friends again.}$$

Developed by Jane Wimer, St. Xavier University's Field-Based Master's Program, Prospect Heights, Illinois.

Figure 6.9b

ASKING STUDENTS TO INVOKE PERSONAL FEELINGS

A natural extension of asking students to become personally involved in their reading is to ask them to invoke their personal reactions to what they read. Rather than merely requiring them to report facts, students need to be encouraged to create meaning from a text based on prior knowledge, personal experiences, and emotional needs. In order to understand a text, a reader needs to make connections with the materials in it (Probst 1987). Since readers have different backgrounds, interests, attitudes, and experiences, they also understand and interpret texts in different ways. In fact, the act of reading itself can confirm or reshape a reader's ideas and beliefs (Probst 1987). By asking readers to respond to what they read, teachers can discover how students think when they read and thus gain insight into the individual's thoughts, feelings, and opinions about the reading.

I can't believe my gym teacher is making me keep a journal about sit-ups.

Requiring students to write their reactions to a text takes time. A teacher can encourage student responses by asking them to note their thoughts, reactions, questions, or concerns about their reading. Then students can share all or part of what they have written, listen to others, and react to what they wrote and heard (Probst 1987). In essence, the writing and sharing process encourages discussion of a text from the reader's point of view and makes the reading more personal. Thus, after reading about the Great Depression, students might be asked to consider the facts in light of these questions: What part of the chapter did you find most interesting or thought provoking? Which part of the chapter distressed you the most or made you the happiest? Can you see any parallels between the times of the Great Depression and your own life or situation? What facts of the Depression would you share with your younger brother? Your girlfriend? Your boyfriend? Why did you choose those facts? If you could change just one historical event or fact during the Great Depression, what would you change and why? If you could help one group or person who suffered the effects of the Great Depression, who would it be, and how would you help? Following are three strategies that ask students to invoke personal feelings.

Possible Dialogues

Conversation is an integral part of our lives. When we talk to other people, we exchange our ideas, thoughts, questions, and feelings. To write a Possible Dialogue (Beaman 1985), students need to reexamine their text(s) to choose pertinent facts and ideas in order to create a conversation with the author, an important person, or an imagined character who can relate to main events or concepts in the content. In addition, students must assume another viewpoint; thus, they become the author or person in the text and think as that individual does as they write the conversation. Students will have a better understanding of what they read as they "become" the content and create a "real-life" conversation, making the content material realistic and connecting it to their own lives. This strategy fosters the verbal/linguistic, logical/mathematical, intrapersonal, and interpersonal intelligences.

 Steps for Possible Dialogues

1. Tell students to examine a text(s) for facts and ideas about a content area topic.
2. Ask them to list or think about key facts and ideas from the passage.
3. Emphasize that students need to determine a specific viewpoint for their information.
4. Explain that they will write from a specific viewpoint in the form of a dialogue with another person.
5. After the teacher models the strategy, students can then use it independently.

This strategy has its place in any content area. We suggest the following uses: in social studies, Thomas Jefferson and John Hancock can discuss the Declaration of Independence, or a survivor of the Holocaust can discuss her experiences with a friend; in mathematics, a banker can explain different interest rates to a customer; in language arts, Henry W. Longfellow and James R. Lowell can discuss elements of romanticism; in art, an architect can explain the elements of her design to a client. Figure 6.10 provides a Possible Dialogue for science.

Possible Dialogue for Science

Customer:	I want to find some flowers that will flourish and spread. quickly so I won't have to buy too many plants. Do you have any suggestions?
Nursery Clerk:	You might want to buy some salvia; they reproduce easily.
Customer:	I don't remember my biology. Would you explain how they multiply?
Nursery Clerk:	Sure. An insect enters the flower and pushes against the short anther, the organ that discharges the pollen. This causes the longer anther to descend and touch the insect. The insect then takes the pollen and deposits it into the stamen, which is at the center of another flower. As a result, the flower reproduces.
Customer:	Thanks for the lesson. I'll buy five plants and let you know what happens.

Figure 6.10

Journals and Learning Logs

Journal writing allows students to increase fluency, use note taking and documentation skills, and develop vocabulary and writing skills. Since writing in a journal is usually less structured and less formal than most other writing, students are generally receptive to its use. Using a journal, learning log, or notebook in the classroom is also an effective way to invite students to respond, reflect, question, and react to the material in their texts. The students' writing reveals the way they think; therefore, it becomes a vehicle for learning the content as well as a vehicle for discussion (Zemelman and Daniels 1988). Furthermore, journals help develop the verbal/linguistic, logical/mathematical, intrapersonal, and interpersonal intelligences.

Variation: Double-Entry Journal

The Double-Entry Journal (Vaughn 1990) specifically connects to the text and asks students to think about what they read. When students write a double-entry journal, they use note taking and documentation skills to record the information from the text. They have to think about the content and their reactions to it in order to respond to the text, thus making them independently responsible for the text and its possible meaning(s). This journal also provides a vehicle for discussion and further instruction.

 Steps for the Double-Entry Journal

1. Direct students to read parts or pages of a chapter in a text.

2. Instruct them to record key ideas, passages, or quotes and the page number from the text on the left-hand side of the page.

3. Have students use the right-hand side of the page to respond to each item that interests or puzzles them. They can record their own ideas, feelings, questions, and concerns.

Figure 6.11 gives an example of a Double-Entry Journal for social studies.

Double-Entry Journal for Social Studies	
Key Ideas: Winston Churchill	**Response: The Battle of Britain**
Churchill contributed to the Battle of Britain when he appointed Lord Beaverbrook as Master of Aircraft production (p. 218).	Churchill must have been aware of Beaverbrook's skills and leadership in order to give him this command. I wondered whether they had a personal relationship.
Churchill's determination persuaded the people that the war could be continued after the fall of France and then mobilized them into their own defense (p. 218).	What factors led him to be so confident? How did he go about mobilizing the troops? How successful was he?
By the end of 1940, he had convinced the British that they defeated Hitler by their efforts (p. 219).	Churchill was obviously a powerful influence on the people. The British were nowhere near defeating Hitler at this point.

Figure 6.11

Biography Poem

See Teacher Tips at the end of this chapter for a Blackline Master to use with this strategy (Figure 6.18).

The Biography Poem (Gere 1985) is an effective after reading strategy for writing that requires students to focus on important concepts of a topic and follow a formula to compose a biographic poem featuring certain concepts. Its beauty lies in the fact that students must synthesize what they have learned about a subject from a vast amount of written material into a relatively short poetic format (Vacca and Vacca 1996). Furthermore, the formula provided by Gere does much to reduce the anxiety students often feel when they are faced with writing a poem.

This strategy offers students many advantages. It allows students to consolidate, integrate, and synthesize new information. In addition, it encourages active thinking and reflecting since students must process information read rather than merely write answers to questions. This strategy fosters verbal/linguistic, visual/spatial, and intrapersonal intelligences.

Steps for a Biography Poem

1. Model the procedure for students using themselves as the topic of the poem.

2. Ask students to think about what makes them special and to make a list of words that could describe them.

3. Using the formula shown in the following Biography Poem, have students use the words to make a poem about themselves.

4. Once students have written a poem about themselves, they can use the formula or an adaptation of it to apply to any content area topic.

5. To foster multiple intelligences, students can illustrate the poem with a picture or photograph, or play a favorite musical piece as they read their poem.

Figures 6.12a and 6.12b give examples of Biography poems in two important content areas.

Biography Poem for Social Studies	
Topic _____ *Illinois* _____	
Four traits that describe the topic:	Long, thin, flat, state
Relative (brother, sister, daughter, etc.) of:	Relative of Wisconsin and Indiana
Lover of (list three things, people):	Lover of cardinals, Lincoln, violets
Who feels (list three items):	Who feels thrilled during state fair, proud of Chicago, in awe of O'Hare Airport
Who needs:	Who needs to feel the Lake Michigan breeze, to see the Magnificent Mile, to walk across the prairies
Who fears:	Who fears a rising crime rate, going into debt, a farm economy in decline
Who gives:	Who gives state aid to the needy, support to its governor, education to its students
Who would like to see:	Who would like to see state test scores go up, homelessness go away, a third airport built
Resident of:	The United States
Last name:	The Prairie State

Figure 6.12a

Adapted Biography Poems for Science	
POEM 1	
Topic	Sea Breeze
Two adjectives	Cool, sharp
Three verbs or adverbs	Howling, nipping, gusting
Two adjectives	Frigid, crisp
Topic	Sea Breeze
POEM 2	
Topic	Land Breeze
Two adjectives	Warm, balmy
Three descriptive phrases	Coming from the sea; warm air rising; cool air rushing in
Topic	Land Breeze

Developed by Sheryl Silkaitis, Mannheim Middle School, Melrose Park, Illinois.

Figure 6.12b

This strategy can be used in any content area. In mathematics, the poem may feature geometric figures or mathematicians; in science, it can profile photosynthesis, chemical reactions, or body systems and organs; in language arts, the subject may be characters in a novel or short story or a real person in a biography or autobiography; in social studies, students can write about historical figures, eras, wars, states, or countries; in fine arts, students can portray works of art or music, composers, artists, and styles of music and art.

CHAPTER SUMMARY

Chapter 6 emphasized the importance of integrating reading and writing in the content areas. Characteristics of effective readers and writers were described, and several strategies to foster these characteristics were discussed.

COMPUTER CONNECTIONS

1. To practice the GIST strategy, assign students to five or six small groups and provide an expository selection of five to six paragraphs. Each group reads the selection and completes the first step of the GIST procedure, entering their twenty words or less summary in a computer file. Each group then moves to another computer, evaluates the summary written by the first group, and proceeds to complete step two of the GIST procedure, making any additions or corrections to the previous paragraph. This process continues until all five or six paragraphs have been summarized. When the groups reach their original spot, the summaries are read aloud and evaluated by the class for accuracy and efficiency.

2. Assign students partners. Then, individually, have each partner create a Possible Dialogue for a section of the chapter assigned by the teacher or about a topic being studied. The dialogues should be created as an e-mail file. When completed, the e-mail should be sent to the student's partner, who then responds to the dialogue sent. This exchange continues until their conversation reaches a viable conclusion. The e-mails can be stored, and new dialogues can be initiated with other students at a later time.

Teacher Tips

❶ Have students brainstorm different perspectives that can be taken when reading a textbook selection. Make a collection of these differing perspectives to use when assigning the Reading from Different Perspectives strategy for students to complete.

❷ Have students brainstorm different controversial questions that can be used when discussing a textbook selection or a discussion topic. Make a collection of these questions to use when assigning the Discussion Web Strategy for students to complete.

❸ Have students brainstorm different roles, audiences, and formats that can be used when reading a textbook selection. Make a collection of these differing viewpoints to use when assigning a RAFT strategy for students to complete.

❹ Use the Blackline Masters provided for the following strategies:

    a.   Reader's Questions (Figure 6.13)

    b.   KWL Plus (Figure 6.14)

    c.   KND (Figure 6.15)

    d.   Reading from Different Perspectives (Figure 6.16)

    e.   Discussion Web (Figure 6.17)

    f.   Biography Poem (Figure 6.18)

Reader's Questions for

_____

Directions: Complete the chart by providing information about a famous person. Write your facts in the correct column.

1. Who (is the person and who were other key people in this individual's life)?
2. When and Where (did the person live, travel, or become successful)?
3. What (were the person's beliefs)?
4. How (did this person solve problems, relate with others, achieve recognition)?
5. Why (was the person important)?

WHO :				
WHEN AND WHERE (time and place)	**WHAT (beliefs)**	**WHAT (problems)**	**HOW (solutions)**	**WHY (was person important)**

Figure 6.13

KWL Plus

Directions: Record what you know or think you know about a topic in the **K** (Know) column of the graphic organizer. Write your own questions about what you want to know about the topic in the **W** (Want to Know) portion of the organizer. Look for answers to the questions you wrote as you read the material. After you have read the material, write information you learned about the topic in the **L** (Learned) section of the organizer. Categorize the information you have learned, and record it in the graphic organizer section entitled Categories of Information We Expect to Use.

K (Know)	W (Want to Know)	L (Learned)

Categories of Information We Expect To Use

Based on Carr and Ogle (1987).

Figure 6.14

KND Chart

Directions: List facts that you **know** about the topic and write them in the (**K**) column. Next, generate questions about what you **need** to know about the topic and record them in the (**N**) column. Then make a list of things you need to **do** (**D**) to answer your questions.

Topic_____

What Do We Know? (K)	What Do We Need To Know? (N)	What Do We Need To Do? (D)
1.	1.	1.
2.	2.	2.
3.	3.	3.
4.	4.	4.
5.	5.	5.

Based on Fogarty (1997).

Figure 6.15

Reading from Different Perspectives for _____

Directions: Write the name of the article that you will read in the space provided. Record the perspective you have on the topic in the appropriate place on the organizer. Reread the selection to determine possible needs and concerns that might arise to someone holding this perspective. After you identify these needs and concerns, reread the selection to locate specific details that substantiate the noted needs and concerns. Write your personal reaction to the details in the space provided. Last of all, write a summary of your perspective in a position statement.

ARTICLE/TEXT/TOPIC:
FROM THE PERSPECTIVE OF:

NEEDS	CONCERNS

SUPPORT and PERSONAL REACTIONS

Text Support Statements	My Reactions

SUMMARY POSITION STATEMENT

Based on McNeil (1984).

Figure 6.16

Discussion Web

1. Think about the position statement and fill in the graphic organizer.
2. For every YES reason, you must fill in a NO reason and vice versa.
3. Meet with a partner and compare/contrast the evidence you give for each side of the question.
4. Reach consensus on whether you agree or disagree with the question and choose ONE reason that best supports your decision.
5. Next, join another pair and reach a consensus. Again choose ONE reason from lists you have made.
6. Report your decision to the class.

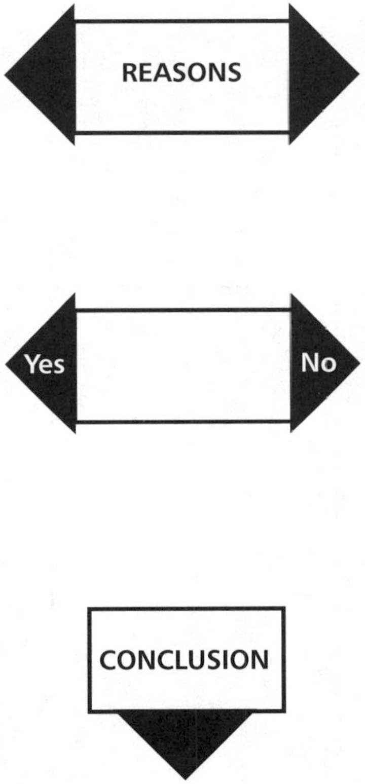

Reasons Against

1.
2.
3.
4.
5.
6.

REASONS

No

Yes

CONCLUSION

Reasons For

1.
2.
3.
4.
5.
6.

What was your group's consensus? _____

What was your *personal* opinion? _____

Based on Alvermann (1991).

Figure 6.17

SkyLight Professional Development

Biography Poem

Directions: Think about what makes you special. Make a list of words to describe yourself. Then, using the recipe below, use these words to make up a poem about yourself.

Or, you can also use this biography poem template to write about another person or some aspect of a content area. You may want to illustrate your poem with a picture or photograph or play music as you read your poem.

Topic _____

Four traits to describe the topic:	
Relative of:	
Lover of (list three things):	1. 2. 3.
Who feels (list three items):	1. 2. 3.
Who needs:	
Who fears:	
Who gives:	
Who would like to see:	
Resident of:	
Last name:	

Figure 6.18

Assessing Reading and Writing

A man is but what he knoweth . . .

Sir Francis Bacon

FORMAL ASSESSMENTS IN READING

FORMAL ASSESSMENTS IN WRITING
- Holistic Scoring
- Analytical Scoring

ALTERNATIVE ASSESSMENTS
- Reading and Writing Interest Inventories
- Journals
- Portfolios
- Projects as Assessments
- Performance Assessments

TEST TAKING STRATEGIES
- Tips for Effective Time Management
- Tips for Answering Multiple Choice Questions
- Tips for Answering True-False Questions
- Tips for Answering Matching Questions

STUDY STRATEGIES FOR GOOD TEST PERFORMANCE
- Test Taking Strategy Outline
- PORPE: An Essay Writing Strategy

CHAPTER SUMMARY

Creating the
Framework
for Reading

Setting the
Framework
for Writing

Keying into
Vocabulary

Strategies for
Comprehension

Research
Writing

Integrating
Reading and
Writing in
the Classroom

*Assessing
Reading
and Writing*

In this age of accountability, everyone is concerned with assessment, and we are asked to assess with vigor. As a result, the use of standardized, norm-referenced assessment measures is on the rise, as is state minimum competency testing. However, as classroom teachers, we know that sometimes the assessments given do not always match the curriculum we are teaching, so the assessment dilemma grows even cloudier. To help clarify this dilemma, we need to understand that tests are really nothing more than a method of systematically collecting information about our students. We can then use this data to plan curricula to help improve students' literacy levels (Lapp, Flood, and Farnan 1996). We also need to understand the different types of assessments, when to use them, and how to interpret them.

FORMAL ASSESSMENTS IN READING

When we speak of formal assessments, we usually mean standardized tests. Most educational settings utilize two types of standardized tests: achievement tests and diagnostic tests. Achievement tests are often used to measure students' progress in a given subject as well as to monitor the success of the instructional program. Basically, these tests measure how well students have learned what they have been taught, but they do not explain how or why the students performed or failed to perform as they did (Hopkins, Stanley, and Hopkins 1990). On the other hand, diagnostic tests are designed to specifically identify students' strengths and weaknesses and, as such, provide a more detailed testing of specific skills than achievement tests do. Secondly, diagnostic tests often contain easier questions than do general achievement tests because they are geared toward the lower achiever (Karlsen and Gardner 1996).

In order to report data, standardized tests provide a myriad of scores for interpretation. Following are descriptions of scores:

Raw Scores: The number of questions answered correctly.

Percentile Ranks: This achievement score, which ranges from one to ninety-nine, with fifty being average, indicates a student's relative standing in comparison with students in the same norm or reference group. If a student scores in the sixtieth percentile, that student has performed as well or better than 60 percent of the students in the reference group. Percentiles are best used when students are compared with others from the same sample.

Stanines: This achievement score, which ranges from one to nine, with five being average, indicates students' relative standing in a group. Stanines one through three denote low performance, four through six average performance, and seven through nine above average performance.

Grade Equivalents: Grade equivalents are probably the most misunderstood scores of all. While these scores indicate the average performance of students tested in a given time period, the earned scores do not indicate that the student can read materials written at the grade level earned. For example, if eighth grade students earn scores of 11.7 on a standardized reading test, it does not mean that they can read eleventh grade materials. In truth, it means that these students have received scores that are about the same as the scores eleventh graders would have received had they taken the eighth grade test.

Normal Curve Equivalent (NCE): This score is a normalized standard score derived from the percentile ranks, with NCEs of one, fifty, and ninety-nine corresponding to the percentile ranks of the same value. NCEs are useful in measuring student achievement that is a result of instruction received. In general, students are expected to increase achievement by one NCE point each year due to their increased maturation and experience. Thus, if a student achieves more than one NCE point, the growth can be attributed to the instruction received. NCEs are most often used for programmatic evaluation.

While we all recognize the need for standardized, formal testing, the wise teacher is also aware of the need to be cautious in interpreting the results. A great many factors influence student achievement on such tests. Is the test an achievement or a diagnostic test? Does the test have the appropriate norms for your students? Were your students affected by any physical or mental factors such as lack of sleep, emotional problems at home, or fear of school on the day of the test? Was the test timed, and did that time factor affect the score of a slow, methodical thinker? What is the attendance record of the students who took the test? Could poor attendance affect scores? What is the reading ability of the students who took the test? Could students' reading abilities have affected their scores? Above all, as good teachers, we must remember that a standardized test score is merely a portrait of a student's achievement on a single day of his or her life on a single test. On another day or by taking another test a student might offer up an entirely different portrait!

FORMAL ASSESSMENTS IN WRITING

Early in the school year, Sharon Thiese asks her students to help her create a list of elements that make up good writing. They usually come up with a list that includes some of the following components: identifiable focus, clear ideas, effective language, a point of view, and interesting ideas. When she asks them to provide some concrete examples of the elements on their lists, they are often stumped. Sharon responds to them by saying that they are just beginning to understand the complexity of assessing writing.

Assessing student writing is undoubtedly one of the most challenging parts of teaching. It takes an enormous amount of time to read, respond to, and grade students' writing. In addition, while teachers may feel a great sense of accomplishment when they have a set of essays graded, the students may not share their sentiments. In fact, when students receive a low grade, it affects to a large extent how they feel about writing (Zemelman and Daniels 1988).

Teachers need to think about the purpose for assessing writing. If they truly want to help students refine their skills, they should develop grading criteria with the students, respond to and/or grade the process, and allow for multiple drafts (Zemelman and Daniels 1988). In addition, teachers need to be familiar with holistic and analytic scoring methods.

Holistic Scoring

This method of assessment focuses on the written piece as a whole and on the overall effectiveness of the piece of writing. This scoring guide helps the teacher evaluate a piece of writing quickly. It uses a rating scale of one through four, one through five, or one through six.

 Steps for Holistic Scoring

1. Determine the components that are important for writing an essay such as focus, support, style, organization, and conventions.

2. Determine the criteria for evaluating each component of the essay. Describe the specific criteria for each component on the grading guide.

3. Choose a rating scale. Many educators like to include a zero as part of the scale so that students will not receive credit for any parts that they do not complete.

4. Redefine the criteria for each part of the scale. Require students to fulfill the criteria identified on the highest part of the scale.

See Figure 7.1 for a look at holistic scoring.

Holistic Scoring: Thematic Essay				
	1	**2**	**3**	**4**
Content Specific examples, quotes, and details to support analysis	Writer does not use examples, details, or quotes to support analysis.	Writer uses few examples, details, or quotes to support analysis.	Writer uses good examples, details, and quotes; some points aren't clear.	Writer uses multiple examples, clear details, and quotes to support analysis.
Organization Clear topic sentences, transitions, and organization.	Writer omits clear topic sentences and transitions and clear organization.	Writer omits clear topic sentences or transitions and/or clear organization.	Writer uses clear topic sentences and transitions; some points not clear.	Writer uses clear topic sentences and transitions and clear organization.
Style Variety of sentence length and types; strong vocabulary	Little variety of sentence length and types; simple vocabulary.	Little variety of sentence length and types; basic vocabulary.	Some variety of sentence length and types; some new vocabulary.	Variety of sentence length and types; strong vocabulary.
Grammar/ Mechanics Correct spelling, punctuation, and usage	More than 6 errors	5 errors	4 errors	0–3 errors

Figure 7.1

Analytical Scoring

This method of assessment focuses on each component of a piece of writing and allocates point values for each feature. It also uses a rating scale of one through four, one through five, or one through six; however, each feature is weighted, and the grade is achieved by totaling the point values. This scoring guide helps the teacher identify a student's strengths and weaknesses in a piece of writing.

Steps for Analytical Scoring

1. Determine the components that are important for writing an essay. The components can be similar to those used in holistic scoring, or they can be made more specific to target the lead, thesis, body paragraphs, conclusion, fluency, and grammar.

2. Determine the criteria for evaluating each component of the essay. Describe the specific criteria for each component on the grading guide.

3. Choose a rating scale. Many educators like to include a zero as part of the scale so that students will not receive credit for any parts that they do not complete.

4. Redefine the criteria for each part of the scale and identify the weight for each part. Students need to fulfill the criteria for the highest part of the scale. See Figure 7.2 for an example of analytic scoring.

ALTERNATIVE ASSESSMENTS

Whenever teachers observe any one of their classes, they are aware of the diversity of each group of students. One class may have primarily male students. In another class, students might be very quiet. It takes time to get to know all the students and to determine their individual capabilities. Teachers cannot learn that by simply observing them, however; they need to talk to them and read their written work. In addition, teachers need to be able to assess their abilities to understand terms, such as *tone* or *irony,* that may not be included on formal tests. This is an ongoing process, and it usually takes several weeks before teachers have a sense of students' strengths and weaknesses. Therefore, it is important to design different types of activities and assessments to accomplish this task.

I hope none of my students discover that I use the stairs method for grading reports.

Reading and Writing Interest Inventories

Any effective classroom teacher knows that if students are interested in something, their chances of success in that area are greater. It is sometimes amazing to see students who say they cannot understand a novel or textbook pore over auto mechanic or computer magazines and technical manuals—or enroll in a cosmetology class where required reading involves a close study of the neurological system. Why are these students successful with such difficult material but not with the novel they are reading in class? The simple truth is that students will read what interests them, and that interest determines how much they read. Therefore, it is obviously valuable to the classroom teacher to know what the students' interests are.

While there are Reading Attitude/Interest surveys available, such as the Mikulecky Behavioral Reading Attitude Measure (Mikulecky, Shanklin,

	Analytic Scoring: Comparison/Contrast				
Criteria	1	2	3	4	Score
Basics Name, date, class; all drafts typed, double-spaced; strong title.	3 elements missing.	2 elements missing and/or weak title.	1 element missing and/or weak title.	All elements included; strong title.	× 1 = _____
Lead 4–5 sentences; interests reader.	1–2 sentences.	2–3 sentences; weak lead.	3–4 sentences; good lead.	4–5 sentences; strong lead.	× 2 = _____
Thesis Identifies two subjects and points of comparison/contrast.	Does not state any subject or point.	Only states one subject and one point.	States two subjects and points; lacks clarity.	States two subjects and points; clear strategy.	× 2 = _____
Body Gives specific examples and details of points of comparison/contrast in all paragraphs.	Lack of specific examples and details in all paragraphs.	Lack of specific examples and details in 2 paragraphs.	Lack of specific examples and details in 1 paragraph.	Specific examples and details in all.	Paragraph: #1 × 3 = ____ #2 × 3 = ____ #3 × 3 = ____ Total = ____
Style Variety in sentence style/length; vocabulary throughout.	Little variety in sentence style or vocabulary.	Some variety in style or length or vocabulary.	Variety in style and length; good vocabulary in most points.	Variety in style and length and good vocabulary throughout.	× 2 = _____
Organization Consistent use of point-by-point or block method.	Order and transitions unclear in several paragraphs.	Order and/or transitions unclear in some paragraphs.	Order and transitions clear in most paragraphs.	Consistent use of order and transitions.	× 4 = _____
Conclusion Relates to thesis and makes a point; fluency.	Does not relate or make a point.	May not relate or make a point.	Clearly relates points.	Clearly relates points.	× 2 = _____
Length 2+ pages	1 page or less	1½ page	1¾ pages	2 + pages	× 1 = _____
Grammar Usage, punctuation, spelling.	7 or more errors	5–6 errors	3–4 errors	0–2 errors	× 2 = _____
					_____/100

Figure 7.2

and Caverly 1979) and the Elementary Reading Attitude Survey (McKenna and Kear 1990), content area teachers should be aware that they can construct interest inventories that are specific to their content area subjects. The following example shows an Interest Inventory for general mathematics.

INTEREST INVENTORY FOR GENERAL MATHEMATICS

The purpose of this inventory is to find out what kinds of things you and your classmates are interested in studying in math class. Before every topic is a blank space. On each space, give a grade of A, B, C, D, or F based on how much you would like to study or learn about that topic. An A means, "It sounds great—I'd like it!" An F means, "It is terrible; take the topic away—I never want to see it again!"

1. _____ Decimals and percentages (reading and writing decimals, multiplying and dividing by powers of ten . . .)
2. _____ Factors and multiples (factors, products, greatest common factor, least common multiple; chance to play factor games)
3. _____ Fractions (Computation, which means +, -, ×, and ÷)
4. _____ Geometry (points, lines, angles, triangles, polygons, circles; using the compass and protractor)
5. _____ Graphing (Learn to plot points on a graph and create a picture of our school Mascot, The Glenside Raider.)
6. _____ Hands-on algebra (learn how to solve equations using manipulatives; learn how to do what eighth graders know while you're in sixth grade!)
7. _____ Long division (Solve long division problems with 2–3 digit divisors while reviewing multiplication and division facts.)
8. _____ Measurement (perimeter, circumference, area, surface area, and volume)
9. _____ Metric system (Find out how to use it. Why isn't the United States using it?)
10. _____ Positive and negative numbers (Find out more about them—you're already using them and probably don't realize it!)
11. _____ Probability (Find out the chances of skipping a grade, winning the lottery, or having a snow day this year!)
12. _____ Statistics (Organize data after taking surveys; learn mean, median, mode, and frequency.)
13. _____ Tables, graphs, and charts (Learn math graphics.)
14. _____ Tessellations and string art (math projects that involve art)
15. _____ Calculators (How to use the TI -30 X Solar Calculator.)
16. _____ Estimation skills (How to stop making wild guesses!)
17. _____ Games, puzzles, and brain teasers (How to have fun while learning math.)
18. _____ Hands-on manipulatives (using counters, blocks, models, grid paper, etc.)
19. _____ Journaling (How to write about math.)
20. _____ Mental math strategies (How to solve problems quickly and easily.)
21. _____ Problem solving (Figuring out what to do with word problems!)

22. _____ Study skills (How to become an A+ math student!)

23. _____ Technology/computers

24. _____ Visuals/media (watching videos about math, creating graphs and charts, etc.)

Developed by Diane Wilkin, St. Xavier University's Field-Based Master's Program, Hanover Park, Illinois.

Figure 7.3 shows a way to learn what your students want to do in gym class, followed by a handy survey of writing questions.

Sample of Early Elementary Physical Education Interest Inventory

Directions: The purpose of this inventory is to find what you and your classmates are interested in. Place an x in the boxes below the face that best fits how you feel. A smiley face means I love it; a general no expression face means I really don't care one way or another; and a sad face means I'd rather not do that activity.

UNIT	☺ I LOVE IT	😐 I DON'T CARE	☹ I DON'T WANT IT
Beanbags	×		
Line dance		×	
Balloons	×		
Square dance			×
Yarn balls			×
Hoops		×	
Parachute	×		
Cage ball		×	
Foam Frisbees	×		
Jump rope	×		
Fitness activities	×		
Obstacle course			×
Bowling			×
Rhythm sticks		×	
Heart adventure		×	
Aerobics			×
Hockey skills	×		
Football skills		×	
Soccer skills			×
Basketball skills	×		
Ball skills	×		
Volleyball skills	×		
Health units		×	
Scooters		×	
Lumni sticks			×
Scoops	×		

Developed by Kathy Houston with input from Diane Wilken, St. Xavier University's Field-Based Masters Program, Hanover Park, Illinois.

Figure 7.3

EXAMPLES OF POSSIBLE WRITING SURVEY QUESTIONS

Teachers can use survey questions to discover students' experiences with writing as well as explore their feelings about writing. These questions provide a springboard for writing; they can also be used to elicit suggestions for writing programs. Questions such as the following can be used:

What kind of writing do you do at home? At school?

How often do you write?

How do you feel about your ability as a writer?

Where do you go to get feedback on your writing? How does it help?

Have you ever submitted any of your work for publication? Please explain.

What kind of writing do you like best?

What kind of writing would you like to try?

How do you find a topic?

How would you like to be evaluated?

What is good writing?

What do you enjoy about writing? What do you dislike?

Do you revise your work? Please describe your process.

What kind of writing do you like to read?

What have you learned about yourself as a writer?

How can you develop as a writer?

Journals

Teachers can use journals on a frequent basis or just occasionally to monitor students' progress in a complex mathematics or science unit, or in a longer novel. Since journals are reflective in nature, they provide a means to examine how students' ideas, reactions, and opinions are related to the content. They can serve as a means of determining whether students understood the material, as well as a means of dialoguing with them. There are several ways to assess journals that include giving completion grades for a number of entries, assigning a letter grade or point value for each entry, or using a rubric. It is easy to create a standard grading guide for all journal entries by determining the parts and attributes for each entry (Samara and Curry 1994).

 Steps for Judging Journal Entries

1. Identify the parts (or pieces) of the assignment.
2. Determine the criteria for each part.

3. Write the standards on the grading guide.

4. Include the method of assessment (checks, letter grade, or points).

See Fig. 7.4 for a rubric you can use to assess journal writing.

Sample of Journal Rubric		
Assignment: The characters in *The Most Dangerous Game, The Birds, and The Sniper* have to adapt to their situations for different reasons. Choose one of the characters in one of the stories. Assume the persona of that character and write one journal entry or two diary entries explaining how the character adapted to the situation. Relate the character's feelings and/or personal traits. Include a quote from the character.		
Parts	**Score**	**Attributes**
Basics	3 points	_____ name, date, class, period _____ title _____ one page, double-spaced
Content	15 points	_____ write one journal entry or two diary entries assuming the persona of the character (1 point) _____ describe at least 3 specific examples that explain how the character adapted to the situation (9 points) _____ relate the character's feelings and/or personal traits (3 points) _____ include a direct quote from the character (2 points)
Conventions	2 points	_____ spelling (0–3 errors)
	Total score:	_____ / 20

Figure 7.4

Portfolios

Portfolios serve as a means of collecting evidence of students' learning, and they generally include a variety of artifacts that reflect the abilities of the learners. They are frequently used in art classes as a means for students to exhibit some of their work and reflect on their choices. They are also commonly used in English, social studies, and other disciplines and

Since our teacher said we can help design the grading scale, let's allow 30 points for name, date, class, and title, okay?

can focus on a unit or theme of study; they can reflect on multiple intelligences or work completed as part of an integrated curriculum.

The Portfolio Process includes three basic steps: collecting the items over a given period of time, selecting a given number of items, and reflecting on the items (Burke 1999). It is also important to conference with the students during the process, answer their questions, and monitor their work. The final portfolio can contain some of the following items: a cover, a table of contents, a letter or invitation to the reader, the selected items with the reflections, a closing letter, and self-assessment. Teachers can grade each item in the portfolio, or they can grade the entire portfolio holistically or analytically by identifying specific criteria. Creating a rubric that allows more than one final evaluation assures validity for this type of assessment.

 Steps in the Portfolio Process

1. Set a time frame for collecting items.
2. Select a specific number of items.
3. Model the reflective process.
4. Identify the components to include in the portfolio.
5. Create the rubric for the portfolio.
6. Conference with the students during the process.
7. Set due dates along the way.
8. Determine how to deal with late assignments.

Figure 7.5 offers a way to assess student portfolios.

Projects as Assessments

Teachers generally assign projects at the end of a unit. By nature, they are designed so the teacher can determine whether students can apply what they have learned in the content to another medium. Projects include brochures, pamphlets, charts, maps, posters, and research created by individuals or small groups. In addition to creating the written and/or

Portfolio Rubric

NOTE: 4 = A; 3 = B; 2 = C; 1 = D

Criteria	1	2	3	4
Cover Title, pictures, and words relate to writing.	2 or more elements missing.	2 elements missing and/or 1 unclear.	1 element missing and/or 1 unclear.	All elements complete and clear.
Letter to reader Reflects on each choice; 4–5 sentences each paragraph; different stems.	2 or more elements missing.	2 elements missing and/or 1 unclear.	1 element missing and/or 1 unclear.	All elements complete and clear.
Revised piece Includes all drafts; improved content/ style/grammar.	2 or more elements missing.	2 elements missing and/or 1 unclear.	1 element missing and/or 1 unclear.	All elements complete and clear.
Three poems of choice Clear meaning; figurative language; 10 lines each.	2 or more elements missing.	2 elements missing and/or 1 unclear.	1 element missing and/or 1 unclear.	All elements complete and clear.
Personal choice Clear organization and ideas; proofread.	2 or more elements missing.	2 elements missing and/or 1 unclear.	1 element missing and/or 1 unclear.	All elements complete and clear.
Reflective letter Describe skills as a writer; reflect; ³/₄ page.	2 or more elements missing.	2 elements missing and/or 1 unclear.	1 element missing and/or 1 unclear.	All elements complete and clear.

Figure 7.5

visual component of a project, students may need to present their project to the class. It is not easy to assess a project; however, determining the overall criteria and then specifying what is not acceptable, what meets minimum requirements, what meets the requirements, and what exceeds expectations, will facilitate the process. Teachers can use a checklist, a holistic rubric, or an analytic rubric as a scoring assessment.

Steps for Assessing Projects

1. Identify the general requirements for the project. Consider such points as the project's visual and/or written elements and length requirements. Decide if the project is to be done by an individual or by a group. Determine if students submit the project for grading with or without a class presentation.

2. Identify which of the requirements will be assessed. Create the grading criteria for the presentation. Figure 7.6 gives another way to assess projects.

Performance Assessments

Teachers who observe students' speeches, video, or PowerPoint presentations, dances, and music recitals know how difficult it is to assess their work. In addition to identifying criteria for assessing the content, they also need to identify criteria for the presentation. They need to think about general requirements like time, written requirements like an outline, and delivery requirements like eye contact and volume. As a result, teachers often use teacher and/or student critique forms, tapes, or videos as additional evidence of the student's performance. In addition, teachers frequently utilize a checklist, a point system, or a rubric as a scoring assessment.

 Steps for Evaluating Performances

1. Identify the general requirements for the presentation, such as time limit, audiovisual aids, interpretations, and the targeted audience.

2. Identify the written requirements for the presentation.

3. Identify the delivery requirements for the presentation. Consider eye contact, volume, expression, flexibility, tone, and posture.

4. Identify which of the requirements will be assessed. Create the grading criteria for the presentation.

Look at Figure 7.7 for a way to assess your students' speeches.

TEST TAKING STRATEGIES

No chapter on assessment can be complete without offering some suggestions to teachers about how to help their students perform well on assessments. We have found the following strategies very effective in helping our students become successful test takers.

Project Rubric

Assignment: Choose one or more literary works and look for quotes that relate to a theme. Create a poster that follows these directions:

1. Use one or more literary works and copy 6 quotes that relate to one theme.
2. Rewrite each quote in your own words; specifically explain the meaning.
3. Write 1 paragraph explaining how each quote illustrates the theme.
4. Write 1 paragraph that explains how the theme is relevant in society today.
5. Illustrate all the quotes and the theme with pictures and captions.

Use the grading criteria below: (4 = A; 3 = B, 2 = C, 1 = D)

Criteria	1	2	3	4
Copy 6 quotes that relate to one theme.	3 or more quotes do not relate; several are copied incorrectly.	2 quotes do not relate; 1 or 2 are not copied correctly.	1 quote does not relate; 1 is not copied correctly.	All quotes relate to the theme and are copied correctly.
Rewrite each quote in your own words. Be sure to specifically explain the meaning.	Several quotes copy the original form; 2 or more don't clearly explain the meaning.	1 quote copies the original form; 2 don't clearly explain the meaning.	Each quote is written in the author's words; 2 don't clearly explain the meaning.	Each quote is written in the author's words and specifically explains the meaning.
Write 1 paragraph explaining how the quotes illustrate importance of the theme.	The writer does not use complete sentences; the explanation lacks clarity.	The writer does not use correct paragraph format; the explanation lacks clarity.	The writer does not clearly explain how the quotes illustrate significance of the theme.	The writer clearly explains how the quotes illustrate significance of the theme.
Write 1 paragraph explaining how the theme is relevant in society today.	The writer does not use complete sentences; the explanation lacks clarity.	The writer does not use correct paragraph format; the explanation lacks clarity.	The writer does not clearly explain how the theme is relevant.	The writer clearly explains how the theme is relevant.
Use pictures and captions to illustrate the quotes and theme.	Several pictures and captions do not illustrate the quotes or theme.	2 pictures and 1–2 captions do not illustrate the quotes.	1 picture and 1 caption do not illustrate a quote.	Uses pictures and captions to illustrate all the quotes and the theme.

Figure 7.6

Performance: Process Speech Grading Criteria Rubric

NOTE: 3 = A; 2 = B; 1 = C; 0 = F

Criteria	0	1	2	3
Introduction Gained attention of audience; developed interest in topic.	None	Introduces topic	Good introduction	Gains attention in an outstanding way.
Content Materials/ ingredients/ examples; specific explanation/ directions; clear order of ideas.	Several elements missing or unclear.	2 elements missing or unclear.	1 element missing or unclear.	All elements complete and clear.
Delivery Eye contact	Reads speech.	Looks up occasionally.	Looks up most of time.	Looks up all of time.
Volume	Can't hear speaker.	Hear some parts.	Hear most parts.	Hear all parts clearly.
Appropriate Formality Poise/gestures	Informal entire time.	Informal some of time.	Formal through most of speech.	Formal throughout speech.

15 POINTS POSSIBLE

Figure 7.7

Tips for Effective Time Management

Many students have difficulty managing their time when faced with standardized tests. An effective way to help students avoid spending too much time on one question is the Plus-Minus System. When every question on a test is worth the same point value, we encourage students to begin the test and answer every question they know immediately. However, when they come to a question that seems impossible to them, we instruct them to lightly mark a minus (-) next to the number on their answer sheets, record a guessed answer, and move on to the next question. When they come upon a question that seems solvable to them, but might take some time to answer, or if they think they might know the answer with some careful thinking, we suggest they record a plus (+) on the answer sheet and move on. When all the questions have been answered, we advise students to scan their answer sheet for questions they marked with a plus (+) and take the time needed to solve them. If there is time left after answering the plus (+) questions, students should reconsider their minus (-) responses. Finally, we tell them not to be afraid to guess, either!

Tips for Answering Multiple Choice Questions

1. Advise students to read the question stem and then try to answer it before reading the possible choices. When they have determined a possible answer, they should read the choices and select the one that is most similar to their original guess.

2. If the reading passage is long, instruct students to read the questions about the material first. This will help them focus on the information they need.

3. Remind students to be alert to ridiculous answer choices. Multiple choice questions are difficult to write, and many teachers follow the pattern of writing the correct answer and an almost correct answer, and two distractors—the wrong answer and a ridiculous answer. If your students can eliminate wrong and ridiculous choices, they will have only two options to decide between.

4. Instruct students to watch for absolute qualifiers such as *none, never, no, best, worst, always, constantly, all,* and *every.* Few things are ever absolute, so when absolute words appear in an answer choice, the answer is most often untrue.

5. If dates or numbers appear in the answer choices, suggest to students that they can usually eliminate the highest and the lowest choices, again leaving them with only two choices to decide between.

6. Advise students that often the longest choice or the choice that presents combinations of possible answers (e.g., *bread, milk, cheese, and butter* or *all of the above* or *a, b, and c*) is the correct answer.

Tips for Answering True-False Questions

1. Suggest to students that since it is easier to write a true statement than a false one, they should assume the statement is true unless they can establish it as false.

2. Advise students that a statement must be marked false if any part of it is false.

3. Point out to your class that absolute qualifiers affect the statements.

Words such as *none, never, best, worst,* and *always* are usually false while *many, most, some, generally, frequently,* and *often* are usually true.

Tips for Answering Matching Questions

1. Instruct students to read all of the statements and answers first before responding to any question.
2. Have students check off answers as they use them; if they cannot write on the test, use scratch paper.
3. If they come to an answer they cannot match, direct them to recall all the facts they know about it. Through the process of association, they might locate the answer.

STUDY STRATEGIES FOR GOOD TEST PERFORMANCE

We all know the power of self-confidence in the test taking process. Roberta Sejnost will never forget her daughter's first state driver's test exam. Only days before she was to go for her license, the automatic transmission on the car failed. Roberta suggested she wait until it was repaired, but she decided to learn to drive a manual stick shift rather than postpone her test! For three hours she and her dad practiced, and on the morning of her sixteenth birthday, she, her dad, and the stick shift car headed to the driver's licensing facility. For three hours Roberta waited and watched. Finally, she saw the car approach, and her daughter was driving. When Roberta asked her what happened, she replied, "Well, I got in, started the car, put it in gear, and asked the examiner where I should drive. He took one look at me and said, 'Any kid who can shift that smoothly deserves to pass!' and got out of the car!" Her confidence brought her through!

While we recognize the power of self-confidence, how do we instill it in our students? How many times have we seen students we know are competent agonize over a poor test score and lament that they knew the material but froze on test day? How many times have we ourselves searched a blank mind for an answer only to remember it the moment we handed in the test? Evaluation in any form is intimidating; the best way to eliminate the anxiety it produces is to help students prepare for tests in an intelligent and efficient manner. The following strategies do just that.

Test Taking Strategy Outline

Just as we often assume that students know the purpose for which they read, we also assume that they also know what to study and how to study to pass the exams we give. This is often not the case, and, according to Doug

Buehl (1995), it is often this inability to take charge of their studying that can lead to text anxiety and, unfortunately, test failure. In order to combat this, Buehl devised an effective process, the Test Taking Strategy Outline. This outline helps students connect what they learn in class and how that learning will be assessed when they create a study blueprint for an exam.

 ### Steps for the Test Taking Strategy Outline

1. Before exam day, have small groups of students brainstorm what may be on the test by reviewing texts, notes, and study guides. It is important that they identify why they believe certain points will be covered. (Did the teacher say so? Was much class time or text space devoted to these points? Was this information covered on a previous quiz?)

2. Distribute the Test Taking Strategy Outline and help students complete it, focusing on:
   a. Necessary study materials
   b. Exam format (Here they need to question the teacher.)
   c. Possible study strategies they might employ that can be divided into Study by Looking and Study by Doing

Study by Looking; Study by Doing Checklist	
Study by Looking (Students review what they have read.)	**Study by Doing** (Students reformulate the material in an active, in-depth process.)
Review chapter	Create graphics—charts, diagrams, pictures
Review study guide	Organize notes into summaries
Review teacher list of what to know	Predict and answer exam questions
Review homework and assignments	Use memory strategies
Review notes	Study with partner and quiz each other
Recite information learned	Be the expert and say it in your own words

Study by Looking; Study by Doing Checklist from *Classroom Strategies for Interactive Learning* by Doug Buehl (1995) Wisconsin State Reading Association. Reprinted with permission of the Wisconsin State Reading Association.

3. The students then create a study schedule for themselves to put these strategies into action.

4. After the exam, encourage students to reflect upon their experiences and identify which strategies worked best for them, what success they had, and how the Test Taking Strategy Outline worked for them. See Figure 7.8 for the Test Taking Strategy Outline.

PORPE: An Essay Writing Strategy

Just as students have difficulty knowing how to study for tests in general, they often have even more difficulty when it comes to writing essay test responses. Simpson (1986) has developed PORPE, a five step strategy to enable students to: (1) *predict* potential essay questions, (2) *organize* key ideas into their own words, (3) *rehearse* the key ideas developed in step two, (4) *practice* by writing an actual response to the essay question, and (5) self-*evaluate* the response for accuracy and thoroughness.

 ### Steps for PORPE

1. **Predict**: Have students generate potential essay questions based on the material read. In this step, the teacher must clarify basic essay terminology for students (e.g., *analyze, compare/contrast, criticize, discuss, differentiate,* etc.), model possible question stems, and emphasize where in the text the answer is located.

2. **Organize**: Instruct students to summarize materials by synthesizing and organizing key ideas by using outlines or graphic organizers.

3. **Rehearse**: Help students integrate the information from step two into their long-term memories for later recall by having them recite information from the outlines or graphic organizers and provide specific examples to support ideas.

4. **Practice**: Ask students to write the actual response, making sure they jot down the outline or graphic organizer they have been using in the margin of their papers. As students work through this step, encourage them to rephrase the essay question or take a position and use transition words to guide the reader logically through the response. As a final step, have them spot check their practice response with the outline or graphic organizer they developed.

5. **Evaluate**: Direct students to evaluate their practice answer, checking to see if it is accurate and thorough, or if they need to revisit the text to clarify their thoughts or locate additional information or examples. To facilitate this step, you may provide a checklist of information expected in a good response. You may ask students to complete this step alone or in small groups where they evaluate each other's

Test Taking Strategy Outline

TEST STRATEGY FOR:

Current Grade in Course: _____   **How will this Exam affect your Grade:**

Specific Material to Be Covered on the Exam	**Study Materials Needed**
	____ Textbook
	____ Notes
	____ Study Guide
	____ Work Sheets
	____ Homework
	____ Quizzes
	____ Old Tests
	____ Other

Format of Exam (Check All That Apply)

____ Multiple Choice   ____ Matching   ____ Applying Skills   ____ True/False   ____ Essay

____ Short Answer   ____ Definitions   ____ Problem Solving   ____ Other

Strategies to Be Used for Study (*Study by Looking* **versus** *Study by Doing*)

1.

2.

3.

4.

Study Schedule: Exam will be given on: _____
(List study times and tasks you will accomplish.)

1.

2.

3.

Test Taking Strategy Graphic Organizer from *Classroom Strategies for Interactive Learning* by Doug Buehl (1995), Wisconsin State Reading Association. Reprinted with permission of the Wisconsin State Reading Association.

Figure 7.8

responses. Following this procedure helps students become more effective essay test takers.

CHAPTER SUMMARY

Chapter 7 discusses the need to understand different types of assessments, when to use them, and how to interpret them. In addition, strategies for traditional and nontraditional assessment are provided.

 COMPUTER CONNECTIONS

1. Assign students to study groups. Have students complete Reading and Writing Interest Inventories on the computer and share their results with their study group members.

2. Assign students to study groups. Have students complete the Test Taking Strategy Outline (Figure 7.8) on the computer and share their results with their study group members.

3. As a review procedure, the teacher or individual students can create enough possible test questions for a unit of study as there are students in the class. Each student is then given test questions to complete using the PORPE Test Taking Strategy Outline. The PORPE is completed using the computer, and completed answers are e-mailed to the teacher or other students for evaluation. When all of the students have completed their PORPE outlines, the questions can be printed out and used as a review for the final test.

Teacher Tips

❶ Create a computer file of checklists and/or rubrics for specific assignments. As students complete an assignment, have them access the appropriate file and self-evaluate their completed work and e-mail the assessment to the teacher. As an alternative, the student may also e-mail the self-assessment to a peer for review before sending it to the teacher.

❷ To impress upon the students the importance of being test-wise, create a pretest that utilizes some of the test-taking tips discussed in the chapter, such as which words make a response false, which make it true, and what format multiple choice stem structure usually follows, and administer it. Then, following the study of the relevant chapter sections, students can revisit the pretest and discuss their answers, focusing on precisely which test taking strategy applies to each quiz question. See the following example of a pretest developed by Marilyn Payton and Barbara Willson, Willowbrook High School, Villa Park, Illinois.

PRETEST

DO YOU KNOW HOW TO TAKE A TEST?

I. **True-False** (one point each). Put a + in front of every true statement and a 0 in front of every false statement.

_____ 1. All dogs can bark.

_____ 2. Statements that use 100 percent qualifiers are always false.

_____ 3. Ordinarily, a baseball game lasts nine innings.

_____ 4. A warm-climate product, cocoa, is grown in Nigeria, Brazil, Columbia, Venezuela, on the Gold Coast in Africa, and in southern Norway.

_____ 5. It is illogical to assume that Thomas Edison's fame was due to his many practical inventions.

II. **Multiple Choice** (one point each). Put the letter of the best answer on the space provided.

_____ 6. All of the following are true except:

    a. In ARS, two book reports on self-selected books were required this semester.

    b. Willy is the Willowbrook mascot.

    c. Advanced Reading Skills is a semester course.

    d. none of the above

_____ 7. Which characters open Act II, Scene I of Shakespeare's *The Taming of the Shrew*?

    a. Bianca and Romeo

    b. Richard III and Lady Anne

    c. Tigger and Eeyore

    d. Katherina and Bianca

    e. Lucentio

    f. all of the above

_____ 8. Which of the following are numerals in the Reading Office phone number?

    a. 9, 1, 0, 6, 8, 5, 2, and 3

    b. 5 and 3

    c. one of the above

    d. 3, 4, 5, and 6

    e. b, c, and d

    f. all of the above

____ 9. Which month has the fewest days?

   a. January

   b. February

   c. March

   d. April

   e. May

____ 10. Which of the following is not a research project requirement?

   a. brochure format

   b. at least four sources

   c. use of graphics

   d. none of the above

III. **Fill in the Blank/Short Answer/Matching** (one point each). Each of these words may be used only once. Put the letter of the appropriate word on the space provided.

   A. "Noel" D. "America the Beautiful" G. blue

   B. orange E. "Angels We Have Heard on High"

   C. protons F. gray

____ 11. What we need to finish the poster is a(n) _____ crayon.

____ 12. _____ is Mrs. Payton's favorite Christmas song, while _____ is Mrs. Klimpton's favorite Christmas song.

____ 13. _____ a color used in Bear's uniforms.

____ 14. _____ a song

____ 15. _____ positively charged molecular particles

IV. **Essay Question** Answer two of the five questions. Do not use number three. (50 points)

____ 1. Enumerate the holiday traditions in your family.

____ 2. Differentiate between the junior high school you attended and Willowbrook High School.

____ 3. Describe the color of your hair.

____ 4. Explain the results of being truant three times.

____ 5. Contrast the weather conditions in Illinois and Florida during the month of January.

Bibliography

Alvermann, D. 1991. The discussion web: A graphic aid for learning across the curriculum. *The Reading Teacher* 45(2): 92–99.

Armbruster, B. B., and T. H. Anderson. 1985. Frames: Structure for informational texts. In *Technology of text,* edited by D. H. Jonnassen. Englewood Cliffs, NJ: Education Technology Publications.

Armbruster, B. B., T. H. Anderson, and J. Ostertag. 1989. Teaching text structure to improve reading and writing. *The Reading Teacher* 43(2): 130–37.

Baldwin, R. S., and R. K. Kaufman. 1979. A concurrent validity study of the Raygor readability graph. *Journal of Reading* 23(2): 148–53.

Beaman, B. 1985. Writing to learn social studies. In *Roots in the sawdust: Writing to learn across disciplines,* edited by A. R. Gere. Urbana, IL: National Council of Teachers of English.

Blachowicz, C. L. Z. 1991. Vocabulary instruction in content classes for special needs learners: Why and how? *Journal of Reading, Writing, and Learning Disabilities International* 7(4): 297–308.

Buehl, D. 1995. *Classroom strategies for interactive learning.* Schofield, WI: Wisconsin State Reading Association.

Buehl, D., and D. Hein. 1990. Analogy graphic organizer. *The Exchange, Secondary Reading Interest Group Newsletter* 3(2).

Burke, K. 1999. *The mindful school: How to assess authentic learning.* 3rd ed. Arlington Heights, IL: SkyLight Training and Publishing.

Carr, E. G. 1985. The vocabulary overview guide: A metacognitive strategy to improve vocabulary comprehension and retention. *Journal of Reading* 28(8): 684–89.

Carr, E., and D. Ogle. 1987. KWL Plus: A strategy for comprehension and summarization. *Journal of Reading* 30(7): 626–31.

Chall, J. 1947. The influence of previous knowledge on reading ability. *Educational Research Bulletin* 26(9): 225–30.

Chall, J. S., and J. R. Squire. 1991. The publishing industry and textbooks. In *Handbook of reading research: Volume II,* edited by R. Barr, M. L. Kamil, P. B. Mosenthal, and P. Pearson. White Plains, NY: Longman.

Christen, W. L. 1987. *The A.T.L.A.S.S. program: The application of teaching and learning and study skills.* Phoenix, AZ: Universal, Dimensions, Inc.

Cowan, G., and E. Cowan. 1980. *Writing.* New York: Wiley.

Cunningham, J. W. 1982. Generating interactions between schemata and text. In *New Inquiries in Reading Research and Instruction,* edited by J. A. Niles and L. A. Harris, 42–47. Thirty-First Yearbook of the National Reading Conference. Rochester, NY: National Reading Conference.

English, E. W. 1999. *Gift of literacy.* Arlington Heights, IL: SkyLight Training and Publishing.

Fitzgerald, J. 1989. Enhancing two related thought processes: Revision in writing and critical thinking. *The Reading Teacher* 43(1): 42–48.

Fogarty, R. 1997. *Brain-compatible classrooms.* Arlington Heights, IL: Skylight Training and Publishing.

Frayer, D., W. Frederick, and H. Klausmeier. 1969. A schema for testing the level of cognitive mastery. *Working Paper,* no. 16. Madison, WI: Wisconsin Research and Development Center.

Fry, E. 1981. Graphical literacy. *Journal of Reading* 24(5): 383–90.

Gardner, H. 1983. *Frames of mind: The theory of multiple intelligences.* New York: Basic Books.

———. 1993. *Multiple intelligences: The theory in practice.* New York: HarperCollins.

Gere, A. ed. 1985. *Roots in the sawdust: Writing to learn across disciplines.* Urbana, IL: National Council of Teachers of English.

Harris, T. L., and R. E. Hodges, eds. 1995. *The literacy dictionary: The vocabulary of reading and writing.* Newark, DE: International Reading Association.

Harste, J., K. Short, and C. Burke. 1988. *Creating classrooms for authors.* Portsmouth, NH: Heinemann.

Herber, H. 1978. *Teaching reading in the content areas.* 2nd ed. Englewood Cliffs, NJ: Prentice Hall.

Hopkins, K. D., J. C. Stanley, and B. R. Hopkins. 1990. *Educational and psychological measurement and evaluation.* Englewood Cliffs, NJ: Prentice Hall.

Irwin, J. W., and C. A. Davis. 1980. Assessing readability: The checklist approach. *The Journal of Reading* 24(2): 129–30.

Johnson, D., and P. Pearson. 1984. *Teaching reading vocabulary.* 2d ed. New York: Holt, Rinehart & Winston.

Johnston, P. 1985. Writing to learn science. In *Roots in the Sawdust: Writing to Learn Across the Disciplines,* edited by A. R. Gere. Urbana, IL: National Council of Teachers of English.

Karlsen, B., and E. F. Gardner. 1996. *Teacher's manual for interpreting Stanford diagnostic reading test.* San Antonio: Harcourt Brace.

Kintsch, W., and T. Van Dijk. 1978. Toward a model of text comprehension and production. *Psychological Review* 85(5): 363–94.

Konopak, B. C., M. A. Martin, and S. H. Martin. 1987. Reading and writing: Aids to learning in the content areas. *Journal of Reading* 31(2): 109–15.

Lapp, D., J. Flood, and N. Farnan. 1996. *Content area reading and learning instructional strategies.* Boston: Allyn and Bacon.

Lazear, D. 1999. *Eight ways of knowing.* Arlington Heights, IL: SkyLight Training and Publishing.

Macrorie, K. 1988. *The I-Search paper.* Portsmouth, NH: Heinemann.

Marzano, R. J. 1992. *A different kind of classroom: Teaching with dimensions of learning.* Alexandria, VA: Association for Supervision and Curriculum Development.

McGee, L. M., and D. J. Richgels. 1990. Learning from text using reading and writing. In *Reading and writing together: New perspectives for the classroom,* edited by T. Shanahan. Norwood, MA: Christopher-Gordon Publishers, Inc.

McKenna, M.C., and D. J. Kear. 1990. Measuring attitudes toward reading: A new tool for teachers. *The Reading Teacher* 43(9): 626–629.

McKenna, M. C., and R. D. Robinson. 1990. Content literacy: A definition and implications. *Journal of Reading* 34(3): 184–86.

McNeil, J. 1984. *Reading comprehension: New directions for classroom practice*. Glenview, IL: Scott, Foresman and Company.

Mikulecky, L., N. Shanklin, and D. Caverly. 1979. Mikulecky behavioral reading attitude measure. In *Adult reading habits, attiudes and motivations: A cross-sectional study*. Bloomington, IN: Indiana University School of Education.

Murray, D. 1985. *A writer teaches writing*. Boston: Houghton Mifflin.

Nichols, J. N. 1983. Using prediction to increase content area interest and understanding. *Journal of Reading* 27(3): 225–28.

Office of Educational Research and Improvement. US Department of Education. 1998. *National Assessment of Educational Progress Report Card*. Washington DC: National Center for Education Statistics.

Paris, S. G., M. Y. Lipson, and K. K. Wixson. 1983. Becoming a strategic reader. *Contemporary Educational Psychology* 8(3) 293–316.

Probst, R. 1987. *Response and analysis: Teaching literature in junior and senior high school*. Portsmouth, NH: Heinemann.

Raphael, T. E. 1984. Teaching learners about sources of information for answering comprehension questions. *Journal of Reading* 27(4): 303–11.

Raphael, T. E. 1986. Teaching question/answer relationships, revisited. *The Reading Teacher* 39(6): 516–22.

Raygor, A. L. l977. The Raygor readability estimate: A quick and easy way to determine difficulty. In *Reading: Theory, research and practice* , edited by P. D. Pearson, 259–63. Twenty-sixth yearbook of the National Reading Conference, Clemson, SC: National Reading Conference.

Readence, J. E., T. W. Bean, and R. S. Baldwin. 1998. *Content area literacy: An integrated approach*. Dubuque, IA: Kendall/Hunt Publishing Co.

Reinking, D. 1986. Intergrating graphic aids into content area instruction: The graphic information lesson. *Journal of Reading* 30(2): 146–51.

Richardson, J. S., and R. F. Morgan. 1997. *Reading to learn in the content areas*. Belmont, CA: Wadsworth Publishing Co.

Robinson, H. A. 1978. *Facilitating successful reading strategies.* Paper presented at International Reading Association, Houston, Texas.

Rodrigues, R. J. 1983. Tools for developing prewriting skills. *English Journal* 72(2): 58–60.

Samara, J., and J. Curry. 1994. *Designing effective units for primary, intermediate, and middle school grades.* Austin, TX: Curriculum Project.

Santa, C. 1988. *Content reading including study systems.* Dubuque, IA: Kendall/Hunt.

Schwartz, R., and T. Raphael. 1985. Concept of definition: A key to improving students' vocabulary. *The Reading Teacher* 39(2): 198–205.

Seuss, Dr. 1990. *Oh, the places you'll go!* New York: Random House.

Shanahan, T. 1990. *Reading and writing together: New perspectives for the classroom.* Norwood, MA: Christopher-Gordon Publishers, Inc.

Simpson, M. L. 1986. PORPE: A writing strategy for studying and learning in the content areas. *Journal of Reading* 29(5): 410–14.

Smith, P., and G. Tompkins. 1988. Structured notetaking: A new strategy for content area readers. *Journal of Reading* 32(1): 46–53.

Spilich, G. J., G. T. Vesonder, H. L. Chiesi, and J. F. Voss. 1979. Text processing of domain related information for individuals with high and low domain knowledge. *Journal of Verbal Learning and Verbal Behavior* 18(3): 275–90.

Squire, J. 1983. Composing and comprehending: Two sides of the same basic process. *Language Arts* 60(5): 581–89.

Stahl, S. A. 1986. Three principles of effective vocabulary instruction. *Journal of Reading* 29(7): 662–68.

Stauffer, R. G. 1969. *Directing reading maturity as a cognitive process.* New York: Harper & Row.

Taylor, W. S. 1953. Cloze procedure : A new tool for measuring readability. *Journalism Quarterly* 30(Fall): 415–33.

Taylor, B. M., and S. J. Samuels.1983. Children's use of text structure in the recall of expository material. *American Educational Research Journal* 20:(4) 517–28.

Vacca, R. T. and J. L. Vacca. 1996. *Content area reading.* Boston: Allyn and Bacon.

Van Allsburg, C. 1985. *The polar express.* New York: Houghton Mifflin.

Vaughan, J., and T. Estes. l986. *Reading and reasoning beyond the primary grades.* Boston: Allyn and Bacon.

Vaughn, C. L. 1990. Knitting writing: The double-entry journal. In *Coming to know: Writing to learn in the intermediate grades,* edited by N. Atwell, 69–75. Portsmouth, NH: Heinemann.

Whitehead, D. 1994. Teaching literacy and learning strategies through a modified guided silent reading procedure. *Journal of Reading* 38(1): 24–30.

Wood, K. D. 1988. Guiding students through informational text. *The Reading Teacher* 41(9): 912–20.

Wood, K. D., D. Lapp, and J. Flood. 1992. *Guiding readers through text: A review of study guides.* Newark, DE: International Reading Association.

Wood, K. D., and J. A. Mateja, 1983. Adapting secondary level strategies for use in elementary classrooms. *The Reading Teacher* 36:392–395.

Zahorik, J. A. 1991. Teaching style and textbooks. *Teaching and Teacher Education* 7(2): 185–96.

Zalaluk, B. L., S. J. Samuels, and B. M. Taylor. 1986. A simple technique for estimating prior knowledge. *Journal of Reading* 30(1): 56–60.

Zemelman, S., and H. Daniels. 1988. *A community of writers.* Portsmouth, NH: Heinemann.

Index